Penelope Leach is a research psychologis[t] [one of the] leading experts in child development. Her bestselling boo[ks] include the renowned *Your Baby and Child* and *The Essential First Year*. Her most recent book, published in 2017, is *Transforming Infant Wellbeing*. She is a Fellow of the British Psychological Society, a Visiting Professor at Winchester University and a Senior Research Fellow at Birkbeck College, University of London and at the Tavistock & Portman NHS Trust. She has been Vice President of the Health Visitors' Association, President and Chair of the Child Development Society and President of the National Childminding Association. She is currently a Director and Trustee of the Association for Infant Mental Health.

90710 000 348 690

Also by Penelope Leach

Your Baby and Child
The Essential First Year
Child Care Today
Children First

London Borough of Richmond Upon Thames		
RTH DISCARDED		
90710 000 348 690		
Askews & Holts		
649.1 LEA		£13.99
		9781472140036

PUTTING THE
CHILDREN
FIRST
WHEN YOU
DIVORCE

How to parent together
when you're apart

Penelope Leach

ROBINSON

ROBINSON

First published in Great Britain in 2018 by Robinson

Copyright © Penelope Leach, 2018

1 3 5 7 9 10 8 6 4 2

The moral right of the author has been asserted.

All rights reserved.
No part of this publication may be reproduced, stored in a retrieval system, or
transmitted, in any form, or by any means, without the prior permission in
writing of the publisher, nor be otherwise circulated in any form of binding or
cover other than that in which it is published and without a similar condition
including this condition being imposed on the subsequent purchaser.

A CIP catalogue record for this book is available from the British Library

ISBN: 978-1-47214-003-6

Typeset in Scala by TW Type, Cornwall
Printed and bound in Great Britain by CPI Group (UK) Ltd, Croydon CR0 4YY

Papers used by Robinson are from well-managed forests and other
responsible sources

Robinson
An imprint of
Little, Brown Book Group
Carmelite House
50 Victoria Embankment
London EC4Y 0DZ

An Hachette UK Company
www.hachette.co.uk

www.littlebrown.co.uk

CONTENTS

INTRODUCTION

If you are separating, getting a divorce or seriously considering it, you're not alone; you're not even in a minority. So many parents separate, from formal marriages, from living together or from civil partnerships, that in the English-speaking world today fewer than half of all children celebrate their sixteenth birthdays with their parents still living together.

Tradition has it that marriage should last 'until death do us part', but in the modern Western world, where an average lifetime exceeds seventy years and many pass eighty, it's often divorce rather than death that ends marriages. One-third of couples who married in 1995 divorced before their fifteenth wedding anniversary in 2010. Half of those couples had a child or children under sixteen, two-thirds of those children were under eleven and more than a fifth were under five.

FACTS

Divorce Statistics from the UK

Based on UK government statistics for 2010 it is estimated that 42 per cent of all marriages end in divorce. The highest divorce percentages (well over 50 per cent) are between the fourth and eighth years of marriage. That peak begins to drop around the tenth anniversary and slows further by the twentieth anniversary. The lowest percentages are among the longest-lasting marriages, 16 per cent of which reach their sixtieth anniversary.

Figures from the UK Office of National Statistics

The social organisation of most societies in the West is still based on families, interlinked through marriages, although the statistics above make it clear that maintaining a good marriage against the social and sexual pressures and long duration of modern life is very difficult indeed.

The only alternative that has emerged into social acceptability is cohabitation, which is not always very different from marriage and often precedes it. There is some research – and political comment – suggesting that cohabitation is not as stable or as lasting as marriage. It is also suggested that having parents who live together rather than being married is a disadvantage to children. Those findings, though, fail to distinguish between children who were planned within and born to cohabiting parents and unplanned children born to single mothers who later set up home with someone who was not the father.

When a marriage ends, so does the married couple's relationship, but when cohabitation ends it often becomes marriage. Getting married after a long period of living together and having children is increasingly common.

FACTS

Marriage, Cohabitation and Birth Statistics

The number of couples who marry is falling. In 1972 a peak number of marriages was registered in England and Wales: 480,285. By 2009 that figure had dropped to 231,490.

Couples living together, including same-sex couples linked in civil partnerships, are the fastest-growing family unit in the West. Numbers of cohabiting couples in the UK rose by 65 per cent between 1996 and 2006, from 1.4 million to 2.3 million.

Of babies born in 2012, 47 per cent had parents who

---

were not married. Of those 47 per cent of births, 31 per cent were registered to two parents living at the same address, 11 per cent were registered to two parents living at different addresses, while 6 per cent were registered only to mothers. Our most recent figures (2013) predicted that by 2016 more than half of all babies would be born 'out of wedlock'. Some now predict this for 2020.

Official figures for 2007 and 2012 from the
UK Office of National Statistics

According to the British Social Attitudes Survey conducted in 2008, almost two-thirds of the people surveyed saw little difference between marriage and living together. Almost half of this large sample thought cohabitation showed just as much commitment as getting married and that from children's point of view it need be no different from conventional marriage; only 28 per cent of the BSA sample said they believed that married couples make better parents.

Whether they live together with or without marriage and whether or not they have children, it is clear that most adults seek committed partnerships. However it is also clear that there are many individuals who cannot remain content for their whole adult lifetime – sixty years perhaps – living with one partner in the monogamous relationship that is a basic expectation of marriage or permanent partnership. There has to be a way that such people can escape or move on, with as little damage as possible to themselves and to their families. Divorce or separation is the way modern Western societies allow that and increasing numbers of us choose this option.

Divorce is a far more modern phenomenon than many people realise. It is only since the late 1800s that women have been legally allowed to sue for divorce with reasonable hope of keeping their children and their property. Even up until the First World War, a woman who left her husband, even if there was no other man on the scene, risked losing all contact with her children – as well as her 'reputation'. Marital separation was a disaster. There was no way to make the best of it.

Being trapped in an unhappy marriage or forced to go through socially unacceptable divorce proceedings produced dreadful hardship, so we should welcome the fact that divorce is now a well-established part of civil society via family law. However, it is one thing to welcome the existence of legal divorce, and perhaps press for it to be increasingly accessible, and quite another to welcome the actual process and its potential consequences. Divorce is not an easy option for anyone.

RESEARCH

Impact of Separation and Divorce on Adult Mental and Physical Health

In a random sample of 353,492 American adults in 2012, those who were separated or divorced had lower scores than either married or single people on the Wellbeing Index, which covers emotional and physical health, health behaviours, life evaluation, work environment and access to basic necessities. The managing editor of the think-tank Gallup, Jeffrey Jones, calls these differences 'staggering'.

Life after Divorce. Data measured by the Gallup-Healthways Wellbeing Index, April 2012

At its worst, divorce can still be bitterly antagonistic and socially destructive, and even at its best it is very seldom pain-free, even for the partner who sought the separation. If a relationship has gone sour or worse, being granted that decree may feel like liberation; if there is a new partner waiting in the wings, it may even feel like the beginning of a new, exciting and romantic life. But even if the divorce works out well for one partner it will almost certainly work out badly – emotionally and financially – for the other. And however good the separation may be for both adults, it will quite certainly not be good for any children.

Does that serious, even grim, message have a sub-text suggesting that parents should stay together 'for the sake of the children'? No it does not. The more couples can be helped to improve their relationship to a point where they stay together because they want to, the better.

But staying together when they do not want to means an unhappy partnership that is unlikely to make for good parenting or happy children. An absence of love, affection, shared goals or even everyday tolerance between parents leaves a chilly gap in children's lives, whether they are eight months, or eight or eighteen years old. That kind of long-term dissatisfaction isn't as obvious as open parental irritation or depression, or the sexual unfaithfulness, enmity and especially violence that poison many children's growing up. But if the relationship between parents has become joyless or intolerable to one or both of them, it will not be a good environment for their children.

We have to accept divorce (and separation) as a safety valve for marriage and cohabitation. Adult society cannot do without one. But the wellbeing of children who will grow up to form that society in their turn is being put at risk by the way that safety valve is deployed. We can manage separation and divorce better, and with children in mind, we must.

As people-who-are-parents, you may divorce or leave one another, but you cannot divorce and should not ever leave your children. As a family breaks up, the needs of its children should be the adults' priority, not only for the sake of those children's current happiness and wellbeing, but also for the sake of the people they are going to become in the future. It is everyone's good fortune that in this new millennium we know more than ever before about what those needs are.

PART I: WHEN PARENTS SEPARATE, WHAT MAKES A DIFFERENCE TO CHILDREN?

CHAPTER 1

SEEING THE CHILDREN'S POINTS OF VIEW

The break-up of a family isn't an event; it's a process and often a very long, slow one. Even if one partner has physically left, swearing that that's the end of it, he or she will have to be back to collect stuff, to have more agonising conversations, rows and accusations, and maybe for some unexpected moments of nostalgic regret when the toddler holds up her arms in greeting. The two of them nearly, but not quite, get back together again.

This is adult business at its most intense, and with this kind of stuff taking up most of your attention you won't have much to spare for anybody or anything else, including your children.

> *When she was driving she just didn't seem to notice the lights changing, so we all yelled 'lights' when we came up to a red one.*
>
> Girl, aged ten

> *Dad came to see Mum in the morning. Just Mum. Not me. How do I know? Because he was surprised to see me home. He'd actually forgotten the holidays had started.*
>
> Boy, aged eight

> *Mostly Mummy doesn't hear me any more. She just says 'Mmm'.*
>
> Girl, aged six

But this adult business is very much children's business as well. It may be your marriage that's breaking up, but it's their family. You are losing your husband, wife or partner, but they are losing not only the parent who is physically absent but both Daddy and Mummy as they knew them together. Deciding to separate has committed both of you to confusion in the present and, eventually, to finding new ways of life; and your separation will turn your children's lives upside down and inside out. There's nothing you can do to prevent that, but if you recognise what's likely to make things better or worse for each child, then there is a lot you can do to moderate the storm.

In the last two decades it has become clear that when parents separate, children should not be involved principally as weapons in a marital war, but should be recognised as its victims. For children of all ages, from birth into adulthood, having the family split up, with mothers and fathers living apart, is always deeply disruptive, usually sad and saddening, and sometimes tragic.

RESEARCH

Children with Separated Parents: Satisfaction with Life

In thirty-six Western countries the degree of satisfaction experienced by 50,000 children aged thirteen, fourteen and fifteen with separated parents was compared with 150,000 children from intact families.

Children in every type of post-divorce household were less satisfied with life than children in intact families:

- Shared custody −.21 (least difference from intact families)
- Mother and stepfather −.33
- Single mother −.28
- Single father −.49

- Father and stepmother −.62 (biggest difference from intact families)

L. Nielsen et al., *Timeless Attachments; Research and Policy Implications*, Association of Family and Conciliation Courts Forty-ninth Annual Conference 2012

The message that parental separation always makes children unhappy is not one that parents want to hear, so if it is mentioned to you at all it will probably be well diluted with reassurances about children being 'resilient' and quickly 'getting over it'. For children's sakes, though, it is a message that needs to be widely served and swallowed neat. Separating or getting divorced is a bad break for everyone in the family, and you need to face the fact that your children are no more likely than you are yourselves to 'get over it' in the sense of forgetting about it or it ceasing to be important.

Information from statistics concerned with the proportion of families that are single-parent is not straightforward because they seldom differentiate between families in which parents who were together have separated and those that have been single-parent from the beginning or in which one parent has died. They do serve to remind us, though, that many separations and divorces mean many lone parents. There are around two million in the UK, of whom 92 per cent are mothers; 1.9 million lone parents each have one child under 16; 621,000 have two children and 238,000 have three or more.

FACTS

Estimated Proportions of Families Which Have Only One Resident Parent

Australia: one in six
Canada: one in four
New Zealand: one in seven
South Africa: one in three
United Kingdom: one in four
United States: one in three

Examples from UNECE Statistical Database
compiled from national sources

In more than 90 per cent of single-parent families the mother is the lone parent and it is the father who is absent. If it is the other way around in your case, you are in a minority and a very small one at that. It is often assumed that mothers more often end up as single parents primarily because men are more likely than women to walk out on their families, or because it is still widely assumed – by separating couples themselves as well as by society and the family courts that represent it – that it is more appropriate for mothers rather than fathers to take daily charge of children. However, there are even more basic reasons why lone-parent men are relatively scarce. First, there is a far greater likelihood of early death among males, so if a child has only one parent living it will probably be his mother. Second, there is as yet no male equivalent to the 'unmarried mother', although with the use of donor eggs and surrogates this may change.

Statistics that tell us how many families were without one parent tell us little about the reasons for that and rarely anything about what is happening now or will happen in the future to the children within those families. Indeed, we cannot even be sure what 'family' means or whether the way the term is used in one study is the same as the way it is used in the next. Most people assume that 'family' is about men and women having children together, but not every family is based on heterosexual relationships. A tiny but growing minority of children may be born to, or brought up by, a homosexual couple, who may be male or female and married or in a civil partnership. A large majority of children are born to male–female couples, of course, but with no guarantee that that nuclear family will last. For all children there is a considerable possibility that their parents will separate, and if they do the children's subsequent experiences are likely to be far more complicated than those simplistic statistical summaries suggest. Post-divorce, mother, father or both are likely to form new partnerships, and these will have an even higher likelihood of breaking down. A parental divorce followed by even one lover per parent and one new spouse each makes four combinations of parent and parent figure, and each new combination may bring the child new grandparent, aunt, uncle and cousin figures, as well as step- or half-siblings.

Those figures are important because when you are thinking about what your separation will mean to your children you need to think about tomorrow as well as today, bearing in mind that any child whose parents separate is liable to experience a complexity of relationships with adults in the remaining years of his or her childhood, and that these will change over time.

QUOTES

'Modern Western families no longer fit the conventional nuclear family mould. Once-nuclear families may re-form, once or several times, involving and excluding not only various parent figures and perhaps half- or step-siblings, but also their relations. If a man comes to live with a divorced woman who has two children, does his mother become their grandmother? Can he, himself, be their stepfather if there is no marriage? If so, how long must he be in residence before he graduates into that role from being the mother's lover? And if there is a marriage, does he, the stepfather, remain part of the children's family if their mother divorces him?'

Penelope Leach, *Children First*, New York: Vintage, 1994, p. 9

Making the best of a bad job

Nothing you can do (or avoid doing) will prevent your separation from hurting your children but, thanks to research studies carried out in the past fifteen years, we know not only how lastingly important family breakdown and parental separation is for children but also some ways in which its impact can be minimised, right from the start. We know a great deal about what children and young people of different ages can be expected to understand about the separation, and something about how to make clear, day after week after month, that the separation is in no way the child's fault or a reflection of lack of love. Above all, we have real evidence to guide those difficult decisions about what children should be told about the separation; where and with whom children should live and how an absent parent can still be a mother or father.

Information about children in separating families in general cannot be a prescription for your family in particular, of course, because every member of every family is unique and what works for one won't work, or be possible, for another. But there are now at least a few research-based dos and don'ts that seem to apply to all children of a particular age group and in particular circumstances. It will always be worth your while to think about such guidelines;

they will usually be a much better bet for your children than having the two of you thrashing aimlessly about in small-hours arguments or taking contradictory chunks of advice from relatives and friends who have axes to grind and sides to take.

Research findings such as these can only help you to help your children if you make a point of thinking about each child individually rather than as 'the kids' or 'the boys'. Each child needs to be kept securely tucked away in a corner of your mind all the time, now and in the several years it will probably take before you all settle into new family structures. That's much easier said than done, but it's the foundation of all the kinds of help that you can give them.

An eleven-year-old girl, middle of three girls, was sent to boarding school because her furious father couldn't – and didn't pretend he wanted to – look after her and he would not allow her to live with her mother and mother's lover (future stepfather). Her older sister escaped to drama school; her much younger sister was allowed to stay with Mum. This child felt herself to be out of sight and out of mind.

My mum did write once a week, but lots of the other girls had letters and parcels and phone calls and visits . . . I told myself she was busy with her new life. I was glad for her. Yes, I truly was. I'd been so worried for her when she was so unhappy. But I felt I'd vanished.

The easiest way to preserve that vital space in your head for everyone is to make a clear separation in your mind between woman–man and child–parent relationships (see p. 99). That means that when your children are around you don't speak about (and try not even to let your face show) the hurt, angry feelings that belong to your adult relationship rather than your parenting. Your ex-husband may be a complete let-down as a husband; a hopeless provider; a faithless, insensitive man; a right b******. But what is he as father to your child? Not 'ex' to begin with (the two of you may be getting divorced but he's not divorcing the child) and, given the chance, he's very likely not to be a let-down, faithless or insensitive either. One of the things that women who are separating often find most painful to accept is that their children still love the man they call Daddy.

RESEARCH

A Close Relationship with Their Father Matters More Than What He Does

A review of research studies between 1987 and 2007 showed that children in intact families who had close relationships with their fathers did better in almost every way than those who did not. One study, for example, followed 8,441 infants to the age of thirty-three years and showed that those with closely involved father-figures had higher levels of education and more close friends of both sexes, and were less likely to smoke or to have had trouble with the police. Women who had had good relationships with their fathers at the age of sixteen grew up to have better relationships with their husbands and a greater sense of mental and physical wellbeing.

C. Lewis and M.E. Lamb, *Understanding Fatherhood: A Review of Recent Research*, Joseph Rowntree Foundation, 2007

Recent research has made a big contribution to our understanding of what parental separation means to children by not only studying families in crisis but also following the same families over a period of years. Thanks to this large and growing body of work we are beginning to accumulate what most of the research community would accept as 'facts'. Not every point may be true for your children, or the children with whom you are concerned, but taken overall these are the nearest we have to hard information.

- Separation/divorce makes children miserable. Children who are too young to understand what is going on between their parents often adamantly refuse to believe in the fact or permanency of a separation. Whatever you tell them you will probably need to repeat it, again and again.
- Older children who do understand that a separation is planned or permanent usually bitterly resent it. It seems clear that however poor the relationship between their parents has been, children would almost always prefer it to continue. Many dream of, and work for, reconciliation. The only exceptions researchers have found are among the few children who are physically terrified of the departing parent. They, and only they, may be relieved to see him or her depart.
- Children tend to take guilty responsibility upon themselves for parents' break-up. Younger children in particular, unable to fathom much of the reality of an adult sexual/habitual/cooperating relationship, tend to assume that they caused it to disintegrate. It is difficult for a child, whose whole life centres around his relationship with you, to realise that the same is not true of you: that swathes of his parents' lives are entirely separate from him. Furthermore, much of the friction that he has seen has probably involved his own behaviour – his noise or his discipline, his mother's spoiling or his father's neglect – so he easily sees these accumulated small issues as the cause of the crash.

'So what was the thing that made Daddy so angry?'
'Drinking my coke in bed.'

Boy, aged eight

- Children tend to feel shut out by separating parents. Most children, of all ages, crave more attention from parents than they easily get. The more involved parents are in couple-business, the less attention they may be able to spare for parent-business.

*You'd have thought she was the only one it mattered to. I just
kept feeling: OK, I can see you're miserable, but what about me?*

Girl, aged thirteen

- Split loyalty is agony. The children who suffer from it most are those whose parents make it acute by encouraging them to take sides. A few parents actually try to enlist children against their ex. Many more imply, often rather subtly, that any communication a child has with an absent parent is disloyalty (see p. 110).

*I couldn't bear him having to skulk on the street corner when
he met us, but if he came to the house she looked all pained and
long-suffering.*

Boy, aged twelve

*I wanted to phone him, tell him things that had happened,
you know? She never stopped me; never said anything, but if
she came in and I was on the phone to him she'd sort of go out,
looking peculiar.*

Girl, aged fifteen

*She'd ask me to do things, jobs around the place, and sigh
because he hadn't done them before. I hated that; hated her for
trying to make me feel I was better than him.*

Boy, aged fourteen

*Sometimes I'd say, 'Dad would have let me do such and such'
and she'd say, very politely, 'If your father had wanted to be the
one to say what you should do, I think he'd have stayed around.'*

Boy, aged sixteen

She was unhappy, OK, I know that, but she was always sighing: over money or how hard she was working and all that. Every sigh and everything she said was sort of a dig at him.

Girl, aged thirteen

- Many children worry about the absent parent. For young children in particular, exclusion from the warmth and safety of home and family seems horrendous and the fact that Dad left voluntarily is either beyond their comprehension or makes no difference to the fact that they worry about how he will manage alone.
- Three- to-ten-year-olds in particular ask:

  Where will Daddy sleep?
  Who will cook his supper?
  Who is looking after Daddy?
  Isn't he lonely? Doesn't he miss us?
  Has he got a television? Will he watch "Dr Who"?

- Mothers who share this kind of concern for the departed partner (or can find in themselves the generosity to acknowledge the reality of the child's concern) and can offer practical reassurance that 'Daddy's all right' do children an important service. As soon as it is possible, children should see for themselves that the father's living circumstances are 'all right'.
- Children need parents to talk and to listen. Research suggests that as many as one in five parents who are planning to separate are so flummoxed by the question 'what shall we tell the children?' that they tell them not much more than 'he's gone and good riddance'. Children whose parents discuss with them what is happening in the family and encourage them to talk about how it makes them feel, not only survive the immediate shock better but also adapt more easily to the new circumstances.

Do your children know what's going on? Well yes and no. They probably know something's happening because Daddy's not living with the rest of you; they can see when you've been crying; they realise Granny is furious though they are not sure who with, and when the teatime fish fingers get burned and there's no cereal left for breakfast three days running it's obvious that their meals aren't claiming your usual attention. What they cannot know unless you tell them is what it is that is happening and why. Tell them. Trying to pretend that everything is just as usual when it clearly is not will only increase their uneasiness and sense of insecurity; and anyway, since your separation is long term it is not something you can conceal from them for long. Once you have managed to tell them that Mum and Dad aren't going to live together in the same house any more, do find age-appropriate words to tell each child why. Telling them nothing is not an option, because if you don't tell them why they will invent reasons for themselves and their fantasies will probably be worse than the reality:

> *She just said Daddy didn't want to live with us any more. She didn't say why but I knew it was because he didn't like me because I wasn't a boy and I still wet my bed.*
>
> Girl, now aged eleven, looking back to when she was five

The truth – perhaps that he, or you, have fallen in love with somebody else, or that he is more taken up with gambling than earning money for the family, or that you just don't love each other at all any more – may seem brutal, but half-truths or lies will eventually be exposed and then the children will have to face your untrustworthiness as well as the reality of what actually happened.

What you both say to your children is important, but what they say to you is equally so. Hearing and dealing with the pain your separation is bringing to your children can be so difficult that there's a temptation to brush aside their feelings, offering comforting words instead of a listening ear. Don't let yourself be tempted. Allowing, indeed helping your children to express their anger and bewilderment, their fears and anxieties, will help them adjust to the new situation. And the more they can deal with their painful feelings in the here and now, the less likely those feelings are to bob up again and make emotional difficulties for them when they are older.

These conversations are not easy and there is no point pretending that they are. Children can accept adult grief and anger, and once they know what is happening, older ones, at least, will expect you to be upset. If you can possibly manage it, though, avoid making them feel that talking about the situation upsets you so much that they shouldn't mention it ever again. Try to make it clear to them that however hurt you may be, you are not destroyed by what is happening. Somewhere inside you is a solid core of strength on which they can rely, now and always.

CHAPTER 2

CHILDREN'S AGES AND STAGES

How children perceive and are affected by parents separating, and therefore what yours need from you both, depends a great deal on how old they are. If you have more than one child, each of them has reached a different age and stage of development from the rest. Even if you have only the one, she is at a different stage today than she was three months ago and will be different again in three months' time. So while your family is imploding, it's important for you to try not to think or talk about your children collectively as 'the kids' or 'the girls'. Group references such as these imply that everything that is going on is the same for all of them, which of course it is not. Concentrating on each child as a separate person will help you to make sure that you understand, and meet, their different needs and keep track of them as they change.

The three-year-old has dropped all his most recent 'grown-up' stuff like using the potty. He's gone back to nappies and baby talk. The seven-year-old doesn't seem to care about her dad being gone; she's only worried about places and things: like will we have to move house and will we take the cats. As for the ten-year-old, she's ignoring both of us, really, and clinging to school and friends; she seems to be trying to be a teenager.

Mother of three children, aged three, seven and ten

His dad keeps saying the baby can't understand a word of what is going on but I still wish they wouldn't count on him not knowing anything's happening. Words aren't everything and I can see him watching them both when they're arguing and noticing when his mum's feeding him his supper but really thinking about something else.

Grandmother of a baby, aged nine months

Our older kid is at uni and the younger one is having a gap year, so I thought I'd waited long enough; they're too busy with their own lives to worry about ours. My ex says I'm dead wrong though. She says home still really matters to them and they're both really upset.

Father of two children, aged seventeen and nineteen

RESEARCH

Do Parents Always Know What Children Feel?

Recent research suggests that just as parents are inclined to overestimate their children's intelligence or how much exercise they take, so they tend to underestimate their children's unhappiness or anxiety – whether about parental separation or anything else. Special research materials were designed so that instead of relying on parents' reports of their children's feelings, children – between the ages of five and ten – could be asked directly about their emotional lives. The children's answers gave a much less rosy picture of their happiness and wellbeing than the answers given by their parents.

K.H. Lagattuta, et al., *Journal of Experimental Child Psychology* 113 (2) (October 2012), pp. 211–32

Wishful thinking may make you inclined to underestimate the impact of your separation and the horrible strains that probably precede it, on your child or children, whatever their ages. However, research suggests that you are most likely to underestimate the upset of the two age groups at the extremes of childhood: babies and toddlers at one end, and teenagers and young adults at the other. It's much less likely that you will miss signs of unhappiness, bewilderment and anger in the age groups in between – primary school and early secondary school-aged children – because while they are often reluctant to talk about *what* is the matter, they usually make it all too clear that something is bothering them, with noisy protests and 'difficult' behaviour at school as well as at home.

Babies are different. As long as your baby is being adequately taken care of by familiar people in ways she is used to, she may seem unaffected by adult upheavals, or if there are signs of distress – such as lots of new night waking – it can easily be put down to that first molar coming through. Teenagers are different again; especially the post-sixteens who are at college or university. These almost-adult children, who scarcely spend any time at home even if they are still technically living there, may seem too taken up with their own relationships to be much concerned with their mother's and father's. Both of those assumptions are illusions, though, and helping those youngest and oldest children through the family breakdown storm depends on you being aware of that.

BABIES

In human development, what happens now and in the future always depends on what has happened in the past. Your baby is at the beginning of her life and what happens to her now will lay the foundations for the whole of it. She isn't going to remain a baby for long, either. If she's a few months old when you decide that your marriage or partnership is at an end, the chances are that she'll be a pre-school child by the time things even begin to settle down, and how secure she is in herself and easy for you to relate to then will largely depend on what has happened to her in between. So do realise that even if your six-month-old seems oblivious to what's going on in the family, and it's your four-year-old who is wetting himself and resisting going to nursery, or your six-year-old who suddenly refuses to listen to a word you say and shouts back if you raise your voice, that baby is at least as vulnerable to family breakdown, and needs at least as much of your thought and attention as his older siblings. If you both choose to accept that and act accordingly, fine. If you aren't convinced, here's a quick outline of some of the neuro-scientific research evidence.

FACTS

Why the First Year is Crucial
Brain Development

Your baby, like all human babies, was born with an unfinished, still largely primitive brain. At birth he had only one-quarter of the cerebral cortex, the part of the brain whose eventual great size and complexity is what makes him human. Three-quarters must grow and develop after birth and through toddlerhood: amazingly rapidly in the first year; still fast in the second year and only a little more slowly in the third. Baby brains do not complete themselves. Wherever he is between birth and his second birthday, your baby's brain is an unfinished project and, like it or not, completing it is your project. It's down to you. Like the rest of his body, his brain is going to grow, but how it grows and develops and functions doesn't only depend on the genes the two of you passed on, or the physical circumstances and care you give him; it also depends on your feelings and behaviour towards him and the relationship that develops between him and each of you.

People have always known that babies' behaviour is affected by the way they are treated, of course. But it's only in the last two decades that it's become clear that parents' behaviour towards a baby affects something far more basic and lasting than his behaviour right now: it affects the actual structure and functioning of that rapidly growing brain and therefore the kind of person he will be throughout his life.

Although the idea that how and whether you cuddle and comfort, play and talk with your baby permanently affects his brain development is new and surprising, it makes very good sense once you've thought about it. Worldwide, babies flourish in a vast range of environments: from tropical forest villages to packed northern cities, from poverty and starvation to wealth and obesity, and from secure adult affection to impatient rejection. Flourishing in different environments and circumstances requires different brain development, but babies can't be born with brains that are already prepared for any particular one of a myriad possibilities. If they were, their skulls would have to be enormous: far too big for natural birth or for newborn neck muscles. So instead of being born with brains already large enough for anything, babies are born with unfinished brains that can adapt to anything and grow with astonishing speed to make the best of the environment and circumstances in which they find themselves. All this means that babies are vulnerable to upset in their families. What's more, they are vulnerable even before they are born.

A baby's first environment is his mother's womb. From around the middle of a pregnancy – yes, weeks before a baby is actually born – he is affected by what is happening to his mother and not just by her physical health, diet and so forth, but by what she feels.

Developing foetuses and their brains receive complex biological signals from the mother and these signals can be affected by her emotional state. For example, maternal stress can affect the function of the placenta, allowing more of the stress hormone, Cortisol, to reach the foetus, changing the development of the brain and perhaps the epigenetic makeup which dictates which of the genes he has inherited are turned on or off, when and by how much. Excess cortisol, especially over a long period, puts a baby at lifelong extra risk of a range of problems, from being anxious or depressed, to being slower at learning, having symptoms such as ADHD and even having some physical problems such as asthma.

Once the baby is born, the continuing development of his still-unfinished brain depends not on biochemical signals from the mother's body but on her social and emotional relationship with him. His dawning attachment to the mother and her attunement and responsiveness to him is crucial to all aspects of lifelong development: to emotional stability and mental health and to physical health as well.

In the first days and weeks of life, a baby's environment still consists almost entirely of his mother, and his circumstances are hers. In fact, each baby in a newborn nursery is already somewhat fitted to the mother who carried and birthed him and he will immediately begin to adapt to her handling and their environment and go on doing so whether parents want him to or not. A new baby cannot wait in limbo while his mother recovers from the birth or his father arranges to start paternity leave. That's why premature or sick babies in special care baby units need to have parents close by as well as those vital specialised nurses.

Every baby needs at least one particular adult who is devoted to him. If he has no such person, receives minimal or inappropriate adult attention, or arrives in a home that is a place of anger, strife or even violence, his brain structure and chemistry will immediately begin to adapt defensively. He may develop extra strong fear and anger reactions, or intense attack and defence impulses in the deep, primitive part of his brain. If, as the weeks pass, his brain continues to be suffused with stress hormones, he may start to become hyper-vigilant, permanently prepared for 'fight or flight' and disproportionately upset by small things. On the other hand, if a baby is born to a mother who celebrates her, cuddles and plays with her, listens to her, laughs with her and comforts her when she is upset, the connections that form in her brain will be very different. Because she can rely on an adult being available and aware of her feelings, and ready to soothe and correct extremes of stress, fear and anger, she'll be on the way to becoming someone who can cope with emotional extremes for herself and form other close relationships with people.

Attachment

Everyone knows that babies need adult care every minute of every hour of every day and week, and it is obvious that a mother (or someone who stands in for the mother) with a close and loving relationship with her baby has the best chance of meeting the demands of constant caring without becoming bored or burning out. But while there is nothing new or remarkable about that, there is a growing body of evidence of how far beyond the provision of physical necessities and into the emotional world that care needs to go. When babies are born, the left-hand 'thinking part' of their brains scarcely exists. Their incomplete and primitive brains can experience a wide range of feelings – fear, anger, excitement and misery – but they cannot 'regulate' them, tone them down or bring themselves back from terror or excitement to calmness. Unless somebody committed, and sufficiently devoted, keeps a check on a baby's emotional state, keeping him in mind even when he is not in sight, and lending him her own emotional resources, he may be overwhelmed. There are few more horrible sounds than the increasingly hysterical crying of a young baby who is being ignored and left at the mercy of his own unmanageable feelings.

If a baby's biological mother is alive and available, his first attachment will almost invariably be to her because they have already shared the months when she grew him in her womb. However, if after the birth the mother is not his primary caregiver, his first attachment will be to whoever stands in for her, his father or perhaps a grandmother.

Attachment is a two-way street. The primary caregiver (let's assume it's the mother) finds herself tuned in to her baby's feelings and those feelings – fear, for example – produce a reassuring response in her, which in turn produces a response in the baby, which she again picks up and reacts to. The two of them are a dyad: dancers, interdependent. The mother is attuned to the baby, keeping him always in her mind whatever else she is doing, and responding to him without consciously thinking about it. Her attunement is helped by his instinctive behaviours and characteristics, such as clinging and sucking and eventually smiling. It is out of that attuned relationship that secure attachment grows.

Attachment is a survival mechanism. All human beings have an inbuilt genetic predisposition to seek refuge when they are alarmed, with whomever they are attached to. People go on developing attachments all through their lives: to other family members, especially fathers; to adults from outside the family such as teachers; to childhood and adolescent 'best friends'; and eventually to adult romantic and sexual partners. But this first attachment, forged in the earliest months of life to the mother or other 'primary caregiver', is the crucial foundation for all others that follow. A baby or toddler who is securely attached can explore and experiment freely, provided the person who is his 'secure base' is available, or trusted to become available if he needs her. Her readiness to give any help he needs increases his sense of security, and the assistance she gives models for him solutions to his current and future problems.

A very large, rapidly growing body of international research shows that babies' secure attachment to their mothers or whoever mothers them, and the attunement and responsiveness of mothers to their babies, is crucial to all aspects of lifelong development: to emotional stability and mental health and to physical health as well. Furthermore, stress, including the stresses that lead to and result from insecure or broken attachments, may damage a baby's capacity to learn and may, in extreme instances, damage it forever. When researchers compare children of any age on any aspect of development – learning language, resilience when things go wrong, sociable play with other children – the tuned-in-ness and readiness to respond of their mothers in the first year explains more of the difference between the children's achievements than anything else. It is a fact, not merely an opinion, that the more a baby experiences his mother or her substitute as attentive, responsive and loving, the better he will flourish today and the more resources he will have to cope with difficulties tomorrow.

Fathers, mothers and babies

Every human baby needs at least one special person to attach herself to. One is an absolute necessity and two are even better. All over the world the first special person (the 'primary caregiver' in research-speak) is far more often the mother than the father. Pregnancy and birth set women up for the role, of course, as do social expectations, but so do differences in the way female and male brains function. Taking what is known about the human species as a whole, females are better than males at understanding and responding to the communications of babies who cannot yet speak. Of course that does not mean that every woman is better at this than every man. Whatever the genders of a particular couple, one of them will probably take more easily to this role than the other. Within some male–female couples that may be the father rather than the mother, and, if circumstances allow, parents may organise their respective roles accordingly. Usually, though, the mother has the largest role and impact on the baby in the first year, with the influence of the father – provided he spends enough time with the baby to exercise it – strengthening dramatically in the second year. Attachment research suggests that what babies need most in the first year is maternal reassurance and soothing, while in the second year exploration and understanding of the physical world comes to the fore and is supported by fathers' more exciting, more challenging play.

RESEARCH

Differences between Fathers and Mothers

Recent research shows that over the population as a whole, the sensitivity and responsiveness demanded by first attachment relationships is more readily achieved by females than by males and that attachment to mothers and to fathers is qualitatively different. Secure attachment to mothers is promoted by the sensitive responsiveness of their care in the first year, whereas secure attachment to fathers is promoted by the quality of their play, and the way they support and gently challenge babies' and toddlers' explorations.

A.N. Schore and J.E. McIntosh, 'Attachment Theory and the
Emotional Revolution in Neuroscience',
Family Court Review 49 (3) (2011), pp. 501–12

If both of you shared your baby's care from the beginning, her emotional life will be both richer and safer for not being vested in one person alone, but that doesn't mean that you will be interchangeable so that if you split up the two of you can stand in for each other in your baby's life. However closely fathers are enmeshed in their lives, most babies start out most relaxed of all with their birth-mothers, perhaps due to long familiarity with their smells, heartbeats and voices, as well as to the bliss of sucking. More and more scientific research is showing how important the relationship between mother and baby is during the first months. For instance, there is evidence to show that it's the mother's loving responses during that period that raise the levels of the feel-good hormone serotonin in a baby's rapidly developing brain. If the two of them are separated, or a mother is too depressed or sad or angry to feel loving and to offer the baby those responses, his serotonin levels and his happiness may remain low.

By four or five months, babies with the luxury of two available parents will often play favourites. Fathers, rather especially fathers who have not been continually involved in their baby's routine everyday care, may suddenly find themselves singled out for favour because their sandpapery faces, deep voices and exciting play are new and interesting. But being flavour of the day doesn't make father into mother, or into a replacement for her.

If your marriage or your partnership is disintegrating while your baby is less than a year old, you both need to be aware that secure attachment to mother or a primary caregiver who is her mothering-person is crucial to a baby's brain development and therefore to her whole future. Babies who don't have anyone who is really attuned to them, who perhaps receive efficient physical care but not much in the way of emotional response, or are looked after by a succession of caregivers, often do not develop as fast or as far as they might otherwise have done. And once a baby–mother attachment is underway, losing it, either partially or completely, always delays or distorts her development.

However secure and reliable your relationship with your baby has been so far, and however determined you both are to protect her from the upheavals in your marriage, parental separation puts not only the father–baby but also the mother–baby relationship at risk. You used to have a uniquely close two-way interaction with your baby without even thinking about it. But that becomes a struggle if your failing adult relationship keeps distracting you. And keeping your baby always in mind is a challenge when that mind is taken up with misery. There is even a risk that overwhelming adult problems and emotions may not only distract your attention from your baby but also put your attunement to her at risk. Being so much loved and needed may suddenly feel claustrophobic, so that instead of taking her dependence for granted you may find yourself yearning for at least a little time when she needs nothing from you. You may even feel that it is your relationship with the baby that has lost you your relationship with her father, and he may agree.

I'm trying really hard to keep everything the same for him. Like I take him to the playground every afternoon but the minute I start pushing him in the baby swing I start daydreaming. In fact yesterday I went on pushing him longer than he wanted and didn't realise he wanted me to stop until he was actually crying. I felt awful. But then a friend came later in the afternoon and I put a DVD on so we could talk, just for a minute, only we went on talking so long that he dropped off to sleep and he hadn't even had his tea.

Mother of boy, aged eight months

Jemima's four and she's getting louder and louder. Everything she says is a shout or a yell, and the more I tell her to hush the worse she gets. The only person she talks normally to is baby Jess. When I asked her why she said, "Cause you can't hear us; you only listen to the people on your phone.'

Mother of two girls, aged four and six months

We were having supper like we used to do; round the kitchen table; normal family stuff. I was helping James with his food and my soon-to-be-ex and I were talking. It got a bit tense and then suddenly James shut his mouth and turned his head away and wouldn't eat . . . it was as if he was angry. I think he was angry.

Father of two children, aged three years and eleven months

Baby-sharing

Can more attention from father make up to a baby for less from her mother? Yes and no. Because you are both your baby's parents you both need to recognise that unless you 'reversed roles' or entirely shared the baby's care from early in this first year, the mother is the primary caregiver and, right now, hard though it may be for the father to acknowledge it, her relationship with the baby is even more important than his. A baby needs both parents to understand that whatever is going on in their adult relationship and whatever feels to them like 'fair shares' in the baby, the baby's relationship with his mother (or primary caregiver) is essential to his development, and the next months of being mothered will have an impact on the whole of the rest of his life. All the developments and milestones of this first year are waiting inside him. He has a built-in drive to master and practise every aspect of being human, from making sounds, using his hands and rolling over, to eating real food or sharing jokes. But the achievement of each aspect of his growing up is also in the hands of his mother or whoever stands in for her. The more that primary caregiver holds and plays and talks and sings with him, keeping him on track, balanced, interested and busy, the more completely he will fulfil his potential for brain growth, development and learning: his potential as a person. This is no time to be arguing about fair shares as if your baby were a meal that could be divided so as to feed you both. By all means agree to share your baby's parenting through and beyond your separation, but make sure you are both clear that while he is a baby or young toddler, what you will be dividing up is not the hours of his physical presence or days he spends in each parent's care, but your love and concern and responsibility for him.

QUOTES

First Attachment: The Primary Caregiver

'To my mind there is one single "primary" caregiver. A good definition of the primary caregiver is that, under stress, the baby moves towards this single person in order to seek the external regulation he/she needs at the moment. Under stress, the baby will usually turn to the primary caregiver, not the secondary caregivers. In most family settings, things are building with the father in the first year and he is definitely getting a good sense of who the baby is, but the primary bond in most cases is to the mother in the first year and then, in addition to her, to the father and others in the 2nd and 3rd years . . .'

Babies' Attachment Hierarchy

'. . . My read of the current research is that the child's first bond is to the primary caregiver's (the mother's) right brain. At a later point, the 2nd year, the child will bond to the father if he is also providing regular care. At this later point, separation from the father will also elicit a stress reaction from the baby, the same as it would with separation from the mother. The second attachment and separation reaction is thus occurring at a later point in time than it would for the mother. Expanding upon these ideas I've suggested that although the mother is essential to the infant's capacity for fear regulation in the first year, in the second the father becomes critically involved in both the male and female toddler's aggression regulation.'

A.N. Schore and J. McIntosh, 'Attachment Theory and the Emotional Revolution in Neuroscience', *Family Court Review* 49 (3) (July 2011), pp. 501–12

It takes true selflessness for a father to put his baby's feelings, and his soon-to-be-ex's ability to meet them, ahead of his own, but accepting that you are likely to be second- rather than first-in-line for your baby's first attachment will help ensure that your separation hurts your baby as little as possible. If you can manage it, further research will reward you with evidence of the growing importance of your relationship with the baby as he enters toddlerhood, and the overall and lifelong benefits to children, adolescents and adults of long-term relationships with their fathers.

Three further sets of observations – and your own common sense – may further help to strengthen your resolve to fight only for what is best for your baby, not for what seems like 'fair shares' for yourself.

- The better father and baby know each other in her first year the closer the bond between them will be in the second year and later. If you want the closest possible relationship with your toddler, don't go off in a huff because right now she's still a baby and is closest to Mum.
- Forming a secure attachment relationship with your baby and maintaining it when she is a toddler doesn't necessarily depend

on her spending overnights or weekends with you. The two of you can become securely attached just by spending enjoyable and predictable daytimes together. Overnights don't build attachment; attachment makes overnights enjoyable.

- If you are trying to make or strengthen your attachment relationship with your baby, forcing her to leave her mother and go with you, whether it's for an afternoon or a weekend, is counterproductive for you and may be traumatic for her. If she cries and clings and eventually has to be passed over like a parcel or peeled off her mother and into your arms, what she will remember is not the nice time she eventually had with you but the distress of that parting. Next time a visit comes up she will be even more distressed, not because of anything you did or failed to do, certainly not because she does not, in her own infant terms, love you, but because she's reminded of her own painful feelings last time and anticipates feeling that way again.

Babies, toddlers and shared care with overnights

Since the late twentieth century, the enormous importance of fathers in children's lives has been increasingly recognised and more and more men have become actively involved in hands-on care of their children within marriage or partnership, and anxious for arrangements to share care after marriage breakdown (see page 127). Many of the professionals who work with separating couples consider that if both parents are willing and able to look after the children, sharing their care serves both adult justice and child wellbeing. Indeed, there is a presumption in family law in the English-speaking nations that care of children should be shared equally after family separation. The underlying argument is that this is the only way to make sure that fathers remain an integral part of their children's lives after parents have separated.

However, what 'shared parenting' after separation or divorce should actually mean, in global family policy or in individual cases, is hotly debated not only by parents but also by a range of professionals inside and outside family law.

Even when parents are cooperative with each other in doing the best for their children, equal shares of children's time and care are rare. Fewer than one in ten children are based with fathers rather than mothers, and whatever the legal agreement, most children spend more time with their mothers than with their fathers. For children of school age the geography and the timetabling of their school lives usually have a major impact on shared care arrangements (see page 9). The practical potential for more or less equally shared care is greater for younger children – for babies, toddlers and pre-school children – than for older children, and this is unfortunate. Since the mid-1990s, a great deal of research regarding parental separation and this age group has been carried out, principally in Australia and in the United States. Findings strongly suggest that shared care that includes spending nights away from the principal caregiver and 'home' may not be in the best interests of children aged between nought and three years and needs to be planned with caution, and especially with attention to the existing relationship between the child and the non-resident parent.

Who is this child?

- *How old is she?* A three- or four-month-old baby may not be obviously distressed by separation from mother into father's care, as her attachment to mother is not yet fully formed and exclusive. However, while such a young baby may not be visibly upset there is a serious risk that frequent separations will disrupt her primary attachment to her mother and its security. Taking childhood as a whole, older children sustain separations better than younger ones, but this is not the case in this youngest age group where two- and three-year-olds appear to be especially vulnerable.

- *What sort of person is she?* Is she easy-going or anxious? Sociable or shy? Easy or difficult to comfort once upset?
- *Is there an older sibling who will be transferring with her from one home to another?* (See the section on siblings on page 5.) Overnights appear to be easier for young children when they have an older sibling going with them to ease the transition. Be careful, though. While the bond with an older sister or brother may be an important support to the younger child, being expected to be supportive may be an added burden to the older sibling.
- *What sort of relationship does the child have with each parent?* The more securely she is attached to at least one of you – say her mother – the better she will be able to cope with spending time with her father, provided that he can provide warm, responsive care. If the child is securely attached to both parents and readily turns to each of you for comfort, then she should be able to switch between you relatively easily. On the other hand, if you and the child are not securely attached to each other and she does not confidently turn to you for comfort or reassurance when her mother is not there, overnight stays will be extremely stressful and therefore inadvisable.
- *What were the parenting arrangements for this child before the separation?* If one parent has always been the primary attachment figure, while time with the other parent has been sporadic or disrupted or even non-existent, only limited, brief, daytime visits should be attempted until a secure relationship has formed.

A baby or toddler's happiness and security in a divided family and two homes is not down to her, of course; it is down to you – and is by no means easy to achieve. Whatever she is like as a baby personality, and however ready she may seem to be to use a secure attachment to her mother as the basis for security with her father also, the success or failure of shared care in two homes depends on how each of you feels and behaves, separately, and together.

What kind of parents are you?

- *Does each of you have a secure and warm relationship with the child that predates your separation?* If your fathering was formerly hands-off, you cannot hope to transform yourself overnight into a secure attachment figure and competent practical parent; it will take time and practice. Equally, if your mothering was mostly confined to after-work 'quality-time' and otherwise supported by a live-in nanny who can no longer be afforded, you and the child both face major upheaval, separately and together.

- *Are both of you genuinely supportive of each other's relationship with the child?* If you want her to be equally happy and secure with each of you, you'll both take endless care to be positive and reassuring to her when she's transferring from one of you to the other.

- *As a non-resident father are you confident that you can maintain your child's consistent and predictable routines while she is staying with you?* That means knowing what and how and when she eats, plays, bathes and sleeps, which cuddly animals or other comfort objects share her cot, and which songs or stories end her day. Even if you were a hands-on participant father who knew every detail of his child's life until you moved out of the family home a few months ago, you cannot take those details for granted now. Children grow and change, and at this stage in their lives they do so amazingly fast. Since you last put your daughter to bed, Pink Piggy may have made way for Dragon.

- *Is the relationship between you and your ex conflict-free?* If conflict should arise, you should both be determined to ensure that it does not take place within sight or hearing of the child.

- Should you run into problems, even in the middle of the night, you should feel able to telephone for the other parent's advice.

Unless you can both come very close to meeting these ideals, your child will be better off if the arrangements you make for sharing her parenting do not involve her in spending regular nights away from home, at least until she approaches pre-school age.

TODDLERS AND PRE-SCHOOL CHILDREN

Children between, say, twenty months and rising five usually react to parental separation with a mixture of confusion, grief and rage, even if they are not expected to divide their time between two parents and homes. In any other age group, older children tend to cope more robustly than the younger ones, but that is not the case here. It is often children around the age of three who react most negatively.

Early toddlerhood is a stage of development when all children, even those in the most secure and predictable families, tend to suffer from 'separation anxiety': the fear of being lost by, or of losing, a parent. At this age your child's brain is only just becoming able to hold on to an image of you when he can't see you, and therefore he is only just beginning to understand that when you go away you still exist and will come back. In the meantime he naturally wants to keep an eye on you and to go with you wherever you go. If you want two minutes' privacy in the bathroom you have to pick your moment or put up with him thundering on the door.

When one parent – let's be realistic and say Daddy – moves out and is no longer there to do the parenting things he used to do, like read the bedtime story or help with dressing in the morning, he really is lost to the child. Lots of visits in the daytime over the next months, combined with his brain's maturing, will gradually help the child to believe in his vanishing father's continued existence and to have confidence in his reappearances, but in the meantime he will probably experience daily life as a miserable muddle, especially as, having lost Daddy, he is desperately anxious about losing Mummy too.

Whether your toddler is a boy or a girl, he or she is likely to cry far more often and for longer than before and to be extra demanding of adult attention. If the child is a boy, he may suddenly seem to become angry and restless as well as sad. Don't be surprised if teachers at nursery tell you that he withdraws from his former friends, spending a lot of time sitting alone, and that when he does join in group activities he is 'difficult' and disruptive. Some girls react to parents separating in a similarly sad-and-angry way, but many girls cope completely differently. You may find yours suddenly behaving like a very small adult, trying to take care of herself instead of seeking adult help, and perhaps becoming worryingly concerned with being 'a good girl' and keeping her clothes clean.

Insecurity, anger and sadness make a potent mixture, which, in large enough doses, can slow up, halt or even reverse the most recent and 'grown-up' developments of this not-quite-baby-not-yet-child age group. Newly dry beds may be wetted again and the toilet rejected in favour of a nappy. Demands may be made for a dummy, for help with eating, for milk in a bottle rather than a mug, and whenever you go out there may be endless requests to ride in the buggy or be carried, rather than walk. Your child demands more of you just when it would be easier for you if you could give less. And if you do give less – because you can't help it – the demands will escalate.

Even under the most peaceful family circumstances, adults often find toddlers and pre-school children difficult to live with, and the circumstances of family breakdown are far from peaceful.

QUOTES

Learning How to Behave

'Children are noisy, messy, untidy, forgetful, careless, time-consuming, demanding and ever-present. Unlike even the longest-staying visitor they don't ever go away. They can't be shelved for a few weeks when you are extra busy, like a demanding hobby; can't even be ignored, like pets, while you have a Sunday lie-in, because they have an unfailing ability to make you feel guilty. The guilt-trips that come with children are worse than the upturned cereal bowls, bitten friends or walls drawn on with lipstick. Loving children (as almost every parent does) magnifies the pain of them as well as the pleasure. Loving them may even make it difficult for you to admit that they are sometimes a pain.'

Penelope Leach, *Your Baby and Child*, Dorling Kindersley, 2010, p. 523

Do try your best to stay on your child's side. Although she can understand what 'no' means and recognise when you are cross with her, she doesn't yet understand why you approve and disapprove of particular behaviours, and that means that she is nowhere near ready to cope with your anger or disappointment or sadness when she doesn't cooperate. If you are angry with her, she will certainly be upset, but she won't learn anything useful from it because the reasons for adult feelings and behaviour are still a complete mystery to her, so your anger seems to her as meaningless but terrifying as a thunderbolt.

Between two and three, a growth spurt may mean that she suddenly looks more like a child than a toddler, but the saddest mistake you can make is to think of her, or treat her, as more grown-up than she actually is. Above all, don't let yourself expect her to understand that you are having a tough time and need her to be 'good'. If you and she keep quarrelling, think through the last occasion – breakfast perhaps – from her point of view rather than from your own. She didn't know – couldn't know – that spilling her mug of milk so it splashed the sleeve of her sister's clean school shirt was the 'last straw' on a really bad morning. She didn't know that it was a bad morning or what that means. If she sensed anything at all as you raced around the kitchen, late and multi-tasking, eyes still swollen from last night's tears, she will only have sensed your general tension, and although she will have hated it, she will neither have understood what it was about nor even wondered. She doesn't understand much about your feelings or your life because she hasn't had enough experience yet, and the part of her brain that enables empathy is only now developing.

It may be helpful to realise that the difficulty you are having in coping with a child in this age group when you are already highly stressed is not due to her bad behaviour but to your general irritation with her childishness. It will help the child because if she cannot be childish when she is two or four years old, when can she be? It will help you not to decide that she is especially disobedient, ill-disciplined and spoiled, and therefore not to blame yourself for being a bad parent – which is the biggest guilt-trip of all. And it will remind everyone who ever has any contact with your children – from grandparents to nursery school teachers – not to stick onto her the problem-labels that so easily become self-fulfilling prophecies. If your child believes that you or her father think she is naughty and nasty, she will live up to that view and probably come to share it herself, and make sure that her teachers do too. So try to hang on to the truth, which is that she is very young, that family life is especially difficult right now, and that you aren't perfect and shouldn't expect yourself to be, and things will change for the better. You can count on that, because the one thing that's certain is that your child is going to grow older, easier to communicate with and more able to understand.

PRIMARY SCHOOL-AGED CHILDREN

FACTS

School-Age Attachments

'Many children behave very differently with parents in their homes and with unrelated caregivers elsewhere, and the nature of their attachment relationships with the adults in each setting will usually be part of the explanation. By school age, though, most children have arrived at one dominant style of attachment which applies in all their relationships, so that 'a shy child' will be noticeably shy in all settings while a secure child will take his confidence with him wherever he goes.'

Penelope Leach, *Children First*, Vintage, 1994, pp. 146–68

Many five- to seven-year-olds seem to react to family breakdown differently from children who are even a year or two younger or older. In both sexes the main reaction at this point is often sadness on its own, without the anger younger children often display. Many teachers (and even classmates) report that these children are 'always crying', and when they are asked what they are crying about they usually answer straightforwardly, 'I miss my dad' or, 'I want my mum to come home.'

But the crying is unlikely to be only about missing a parent. These children are overwhelmingly sad because they assume that a parent who has moved out of the shared family home has rejected them. Many in this age group are mature enough to seek an explanation for the parental break-up, but only the exceptional child will look in the right place: the relationship between the parents. Almost all will assume that the whole horrid upheaval is their fault. Daddy or Mummy has gone to live somewhere else because they are unlovable and unloved.

It's 'cause I woke up too early . . .

Boy, aged five

I talked too loud. He always said 'hush' and I didn't.

Boy, aged seven

They didn't want to get me from school. I heard them yelling about having better things to do.

Girl, aged eight

As well as blaming him- or herself for the parent's absence, and missing him, your child may also be deeply worried about both of you and will almost certainly be desperately hoping to get you back together again.

That was my nearly-asleep dream, about Dad coming up the path with his wheelie and Mummy giving him a big hug.

Girl, aged seven

When the phone rings I always think it'll be Mummy coming home.

Girl, aged seven

There's a concert at school and I'm IN IT, so this time they'll both come and they'll sit next to each other and then we'll all come home together.

Boy, aged seven

My daddy does the long grass 'cause Mum can't. He washes his hands and last time he had a cup of tea. But then he wented again.

Boy, aged four

A child who is feeling like this is at real risk of becoming depressed, and it's very likely that there will be a drop in performance at school and in any after-school activities. Boys in this age group whose fathers leave home are likely to be even more distressed than girls, however regularly fathers visit, and there may be complaints about their behaviour at school, adding to their feeling that they are bad boys whom nobody loves.

If sadness is the predominant emotion in most five- to seven-year-olds whose parents separate, anger often overwhelms it in the eight to eleven years age group. Your child may be intensely angry with one or both of you during and after the break-up of the family. He or she is likely to take sides against whichever parent is seen as having fractured family life, often seeming to take pleasure in apportioning blame. Very often, of course, a child's limited under-standing of the situation means that he or she blames the wrong parent. You may discover that your son blames you for forcing his father to leave the family home, when the reason you took a stand was that you discovered an ongoing affair. Unfortunately their interest in which parent was at fault, and when, makes children in this age group especially vulnerable to parental blame-and-revenge games.

However angry your child may be, though, anger will not be his or her only reaction to the family upheaval. Many children in this age group are also enormously concerned for their par-ents' wellbeing, frightened about what is going to happen to them and lonely for the people they used to be. Even at this young age many also try to take care of the parent with whom they are living, acting like parents themselves and trying to make things better for the adult.

When we're at school she's all by herself. Nobody to help her with stuff, go to the shop for her or answer the phone. OK, my dad was at work but he was coming home. Now he isn't. She

*doesn't cook supper like she did and I don't know what she does
or how to help her.*

Girl, aged ten

*He hasn't got a proper house or his garden or his shed. He's
just got a little room and when he's not at work he's all alone
in it with nothing to do and nobody to talk to. Mum says not
to worry, he'll just be in the pub, but I don't think she means it
nicely.*

Boy, aged nine

More than anything else in the world, most children want the
family breakdown not to have happened or, failing that, for their
parents to get back together again. But however passionately they
want things to change, they are powerless to change them and,
deep down, they know they are. Furthermore, this is an age when
children's social lives and their desire to conform to the peer group
are becoming increasingly important. Should they tell their friends
about the parental separation? What will they think? And if they
don't tell, how can they explain why Saturday's sleepover and their
June birthday party are at different addresses?

RESEARCH

Confiding in Peers

Findings from research based on data from longitudinal studies, such as the National Institute of Child Health
and Human Development Study of Early Child Care, and
the Minnesota Study of Risk and Adaption from Birth to
Adulthood, consistently show that the security of children's
early attachment relationships are predictive of their peer
relationships later on. Children who have been securely

attached since early infancy tend to have more and closer friends than insecurely attached children, and are less likely to dislike or be disliked by others.

P.M. Crittenden, *The Organization of Attachment Relationships: Maturation, Culture and Context*, New York: Cambridge University Press, 2000, pp. 343–57

Children want to be in control of who-tells-what-to-whom, but they are unlikely to be able to manage it for themselves.

I want Amelia to know I'm sad but I don't know what to say to her. 'My dad's gone' sounds really weird. It is weird actually.

Girl, aged eight

If you are on friendly terms with the parents of your child's best friend or friendship group, offer to tell them what is going on so that they can tell their children. As for the school: the head teacher and school secretary need to know about the separation so that communications from the school are sent to each of you. But in addition, unless the child is strongly opposed to the idea, it will probably be helpful to talk to her class teacher, who is the adult best placed to keep a supportive eye on her and cut her a little slack when necessary.

For children in this age group there is about a fifty-fifty chance that his or her school performance will drop off alongside self-confidence and ability to concentrate. As in younger age groups, boys are more susceptible than girls both to becoming withdrawn and to 'acting out' their feelings through unacceptable behaviour. Children of either sex may also react to the complex web of emotional distress family breakdown causes with psychosomatic symptoms such as headaches and tummy aches. The fact that a doctor can find nothing wrong does not mean that these symptoms are 'made up'; the pain is real but its basic cause is emotional rather than physical. If psychosomatic complaints are a major feature of a child's reaction to the family breakdown, seeing a (sympathetic) GP may help, because the child herself may be worried about her health and welcome reassurance that her symptoms are caused by sadness and stress rather than illness.

SECONDARY SCHOOL-AGED CHILDREN

Transferring from primary to secondary school is stressful for most children when home and family is stable, and for every child when the family is in crisis. Although your thirteen-year-old's concern over the situation may be less obvious than your nine-year-old's, it will probably be even more intense and potentially more hazardous.

FACTS

Brain Development in the Teen Years

There is overwhelming and still accumulating neuroscientific evidence of highly significant brain development taking place during adolescence, starting with puberty. The key aspect of this is the marked immaturity of the neural networks of frontal brain regions implicated in planning, perspective taking, social understanding and evaluating future consequences. This brain immaturity manifests in impulsive decision making, little ability to consider long-term consequences, engagement in risky behaviours and increased susceptibility to negative influences.

Specifically, this body of research indicates that early adolescence (under around fourteen years) marks the heightening of emotional arousability, sensation seeking and reward orientation. During mid-adolescence (fifteen to seventeen years) young people are increasingly vulnerable to risk taking and to overwhelmingly strong feelings and uncontrollable behaviours. During late adolescence (eighteen years and over) the frontal lobes continue to mature so that gradually the individual becomes able to manage his or her feelings and behaviour.

B. J. Casey et al., 'The Adolescent Brain', *Annals of the New York Academy of Sciences* 1124 (2008), pp. 111–26

Adolescence is a stressful period of development, and how your adolescent child reacts to the added stress of family breakdown depends not only on chronological age but also on the point he or she has reached in the developments of puberty. Bear in mind that immature brain development means that teenagers tend to be emotional, impulsive and liable to take risks without thinking through consequences.

Some adolescents who don't like what is going on at home partially disengage from their families and spend more time with their friends elsewhere. This can be a good adaptation or a risky one, and only you two can decide which is the case with your child. For a fourteen- or fifteen-year-old who has already achieved some personal autonomy and independence from his parents, effectively focusing on his own friendships, ambitions and plans and disregarding the parents' problems may be an adaptive way to react to family breakdown. But when a twelve- or thirteen-year-old who feels lonely without the accustomed family structure and is less carefully supervised than before takes refuge with groups of somewhat older peers, there is a real risk of him or her joining exciting risky activities which sometimes may involve underage drinking, sexual activity or drug-taking, possibly coupled with shoplifting or other anti-social or illegal behaviour.

An opposite reaction, seen almost exclusively among girls, pulls a teenager more closely into the family, coping with her own loneliness, confusion and guilt by helping to run a fractured household or to care for younger children.

If you are struggling to work full time as a single parent, your adolescent daughter's willingness and competence may be crucially helpful. But if she is expected to provide tea and sympathy for younger school children and perhaps to complete the day's domestic chores and prepare an evening meal, do acknowledge that in enabling you to do a full-time paid job she is doing a part-time one herself. She is in exactly the same position as she would be if she worked in a family business or as an au pair in another family.

It can be very valuable to an older adolescent to feel that he or she is a necessary part of the home set-up, but don't let yourself slip into dependence on that labour. There will come a time when he or she wants (and needs) either to leave home altogether or to transfer to 'lodger' status while attending college or serving an apprenticeship. It is one thing for the adolescent to feel needed, quite another to know that his or her presence is literally indispensable. When he or she leaves school and finds a job, you must not ask, even silently and with your eyes, 'who is to look after the little ones until I get home from work?' That must not be the adolescent's problem, because it is yours. You need to have foreseen both question and answer in advance. Leaving home is difficult enough for many youngsters without that kind of added stress.

In the meantime, however welcome her help and companionship may be, don't often let her stay at home instead of going out with friends, or help small siblings with homework instead of doing her own. It is not her job to manage your problems; it is your job to protect her from them.

Even in intact and stable families many adolescents of all ages and both sexes experience conflict between home life and peer group life. If most of every weekend goes on sport, the young person may see very little of his or her family; and if every Friday and Saturday night is for going out with friends, he or she will be left out of family birthday celebrations or treat dinners. Balance and compromise is needed. When parents separate, the need for that balance is doubled, but available compromises are often halved. Arrangements that ensure that a child spends time with each parent – such as weekends with Dad – may work well when children are in primary school but become intolerable to teenagers who need to be allowed, even encouraged, to hang out with their friends. But at the same time that they are fighting against having to be away from home base every weekend, many adolescents will regret seeing less of the non-resident parent and feel guilty for not doing more to fill the empty partner-shaped space in each parent's life. Boys may feel that they ought to be 'the man about the house', not only in the sense of changing light bulbs or carrying heavy stuff but also in the sense of looking after the mother if she seems sad or lonely. Girls likewise often feel obliged to keep their fathers company. It is all too easy for such relationships to become inappropriately romantic, even seductive, unless parents draw and maintain very clear lines between adult and child, parent and friend.

STUDENTS AND YOUNG ADULTS

The depth of the effect parental separation or divorce can have on 'grown-up' children is often overlooked, or disbelieved. Older teenagers, perhaps those who are already at college or living away at university, spend few stretches of time at home and may seem only to make contact when they need something. Some parents accuse them of behaving like lodgers or of treating the home like a hotel. Do be careful, though, that you do not treat your daughter or son like a lodger or a guest. The home – particularly their room or space within it – and family members are enormously important to them as the safe base from which they came and to which they can return when outside life gets too difficult. The fact that your child doesn't spend much time in the home or with you does not mean that either has become unimportant.

> *Before I even left for uni, Mum told me she was going to give my room to my sister so that she and my littlest sister had a room each and I could share with one of them when I came home. OK, it sounds kind of reasonable, I know, but I really minded so much, especially when she packed all my stuff up. My dad knew I was upset and eventually he asked if I'd like to make the room I stayed in at his house into my own. It was nice of him but I couldn't really do that to my mum . . .*
>
> Girl, aged eighteen

> *My parents stayed together for me until I'd done my GCSEs and started college. I didn't know that – no idea. When they told me they were splitting up and selling the house to buy a flat each they seemed to think I wouldn't care. No, worse than that: they seemed to think it was none of my business. I actually think that's why I made such a mess of everything.*
>
> Boy, aged nineteen

It isn't uncommon for parents to struggle or drift on in a more or less loveless marriage 'until the children leave home' and then split up. If you have stayed together 'for the sake of the children' you may have given them stability, as you intended, but you may also have presented them with a very chilly model of adult relationships. What's more, the break-up, when it comes, may not be any easier for these nearly-adult children than it would have been years ago. If your teenager had thought – or assumed – that you were reasonably happy together (or hadn't given the matter any thought) and is now told that your separation has long been planned, he's liable to feel that if your relationship with each other was a lie so was his whole childhood and his relationships with you. A late family break-up has an enormous impact on the young person's sense of his own family history.

> *First I really couldn't believe what they were telling me. Truly. I had a moment there when I thought it must be a joke. But then it sank in and it just sort of stole my childhood. OK, that sounds dramatic, but everything I'd known and trusted had been a lie and they'd been waiting for me to get out of the way so they could smash it up. I stayed angry for years. Actually I'm still angry. I'm not nearly as close to either of my parents as a lot of my friends are to theirs.*
>
> Man, aged twenty-two

Try not to assume that at nineteen or even twenty your children are grown-up enough to be able to understand why you have split up and be 'sensible' about it and 'fair' to both of you. Above all, don't assume that because they have sexual relationships themselves they will sympathise with a parent's affair. Young people who are struggling to find themselves as adult men or women are often very judgemental about parents' behaviour and usually intensely embarrassed if they are forced to acknowledge parents' sexuality. You are their mother and father, not their friends. The less you confide in them the better.

> *When I was fourteen my dad told me that one of the things he missed about my mother was her 'tip-tilted breasts'. Even as an adult and a parent myself I can't forgive his crass insensitivity. Talk about 'too much information . . .'*
>
> Woman, looking back to when she was fourteen

CHAPTER 3

OTHER PEOPLE, INSIDE AND OUTSIDE THE FAMILY

Separation and divorce isn't nearly as private a matter as most couples think – or hope. Because our society and the care of the next generation are organised around marriage and monogamy, the break-up of a family touches many people directly. There are close relations and relations-by-marriage who may be deeply saddened for you both. Your own mother may wonder if she is partly responsible because she divorced herself and then brought you up without a father-figure. In your own generation there may be brothers or sisters who are alarmed for themselves, feeling that if your apparently solid marriage has foundered, their own may be at risk. A little further away there may be cousins and perhaps their girlfriends or boyfriends (and their families) who feel personally interested in what has happened and why. And then, of course, the break-up will be titillatingly interesting to almost every acquaintance who hears of it – and many will.

Not all these people will matter to your children, of course, but some will. When parents separate, having other people they are close to around – relatives or longstanding family friends – can make a tremendous difference both directly to the children themselves and indirectly because supported parents are more able to be supportive to their children.

SIBLINGS

The most important people to a child, outside the bust-up trio of himself, his father and his mother, are usually brothers and sisters. During a parental break-up it is bad luck to be an 'only' child, because children come through better if they have one or more siblings to share it with, whatever their ages and the age gaps between them and even if they haven't been especially close up to now. In middle childhood and in adolescence, children may find it easier to talk about what is going on to each other than to anyone else. Where the age gap is too great for comfortable confidences, younger siblings can feel cared for and older siblings can feel caring. That often gives both children some of what they feel the breakdown of the family is taking from them: loving care.

Don't let yourself rely too much on the relationships between your children, though. You are the grown-ups. The fact that two teenagers support and confide in each other doesn't mean that they don't need to talk to you both. And it is all too easy to let the care an older child gives to a younger one become burdensome for her.

> When our parents finally split up I was eleven and Jack was eight and he really didn't like going to dad's flat on his own so we always went together. But now he's eleven he still always wants me to go too, and often I really need to be around with my friends. Dad understands that. He'd be cool with me meeting him for lunch sometimes instead of spending all day, but Jack really needs me.
>
> Girl, aged fourteen

Whatever their ages and however close they may feel, your children are not responsible for each other; you and their father are responsible for all of them, and you may need to spell that out many times in addition to acting accordingly.

Above all, although you can count on simple companionship meaning that two or more children help each other to cope with this stressful time, don't assume, or let anyone, including the children themselves assume, that they feel exactly the same about the situation or aspects of it. One child may blame her mother for everything that's gone wrong, while another blames her father. One may think his own bad behaviour was responsible for his dad leaving, and another, enshrined as the family-good-kid, may thankfully agree because holding her brother responsible lets her off the hook. Later on, one child may love going to father's house while another may find leaving mother intolerable. Eventually, one may like the new stepmother while another blames her for the break-up or resents her attempts at mothering.

You can't conjure up a sibling for your child, of course, any more than you can magically produce an extended family or support network. If there's only one child involved in your break-up the particular things you need to watch out for depend very much on her age. If she is a baby or young toddler she shouldn't be expected to be away from you overnight, though if she has a trusted older sibling he or she might help to keep separation anxiety in check. If she is a teenager or student, her companion and confidante would probably be a friend, even if there was a sibling available. It's during the in-between years – say five to fourteen – that being the only child of a broken family may be especially difficult. Whichever parent the child is with there are only the two of them and it is easy for them to come to depend on each other for company and support. There are girls not yet in their teens who feel that they ought to look after their lone fathers, domestically and even romantically, and boys who try to be the man of the house for their lone mothers. Sometimes, well-meaning but misguided relations and family friends actually exhort children to look after their parents. Unfortunately a lone father or mother is often also lonely and all too willing to step out of the parent role to make a companion, even confidante, of the child.

Of course I knew he was lonely – he was so horribly pleased to see me at weekends that I couldn't ever say I wanted to stay at home for someone's birthday party.

Girl, aged twelve

She used to give me wine because she said she couldn't drink by herself. One day I told that to my dad and he was really, really furious.

Boy, aged eleven

I know she's unhappy but I wish she wouldn't tell me why. I think it's what's called 'too much information'.

Boy, aged thirteen

The more adult friends and supporters the parent has, the more likely it is that he or she will be able to see adult life as continuing even without the partner, and the easier it will be for the child to see the parent as 'OK' and, hopefully, to relax and gradually relinquish the quasi-adult role. However, children in this situation can easily become jealous of anyone else their parent relies on, especially if it's a boyfriend or girlfriend.

I had come to rely a lot on my friend Maria. She quite often came round and cooked tea for us both at my place. She was dying to meet my daughter so she came on Saturday meaning to do a nice meal for the three of us but Rhianna would hardly speak to her. When she saw Maria in the kitchen cooking, she went mental and said I obviously didn't need her so she was going home. I asked my ex if it had been tactless of me to have Maria there and what she told me isn't repeatable!

Father of girl, aged fourteen

GRANDPARENTS

Grandparents are very special to a lot of children, and children are very special to a lot of grandparents. Many grandparents are special to their grandchildren's parents (their own adult children), too. In fact the popular assumption that grandchildren are even more beloved than children does not bear examination. Much of what grandparents do for their grandchildren they do to please their children and be involved in their lives.

The importance of grandparents to families in the Western world, especially to children, is seriously underestimated. Grandparents who live close by often provide the childcare that makes it possible for their daughter or daughter-in-law to work outside home. Grandparents who live too far away to provide hands-on help quite often help financially instead. A few contribute to the down-payment on a home. Some pay towards nursery costs or help out with extras such as school trips or music lessons for an older child.

RESEARCH

Grandparents' Contribution to Children's Care

Throughout the English-speaking world and starting from babyhood, more children who need care while parents are at work get it from grandparents than from anyone else.

Around a quarter of the American babies in the National Institute of Child Health and Human Development study, and a similar proportion of the English babies in the Families, Children and Child Care study, were cared for by grandparents for an average of around thirty hours a week once they had any regular care from anyone but the mother.

By the end of babies' first year, grandparent care is not quite so predominant because other types of care are used more frequently. Grandparents continue to provide a large proportion of the total, however – often a larger proportion than is immediately obvious from statistical tables. When children are in more than one type of non-maternal child-care, the second or 'extra' type is usually grandparent care. In the FCCC study, for example, when children were in what was termed 'combination care' – family day-care, say, plus something else – the something else was almost invariably care by a grandparent. And when grandparents' contribution to 'combined care' was added to the category of 'grandparent care', it became clear that grandparents were providing more childcare than any other category of caregiver.

Penelope Leach, *Childcare Today*, Vintage, 2010, pp. 115–24

Even if grandparents undertake no regular childcare at all, many still make a large – if largely unrecorded and therefore hard to quantify – contribution to those children's care and wellbeing, including the parents' ability to hold down a job. Grandparents who live within easy reach of the grandchildren's home often serve as back-up caregivers who can be called upon to step in when regular arrangements go wrong. Even grandparents who live hours of travelling time away are sometimes called upon to come and stay with children who are too ill for their regular childcare, so that parents need not take time off from work.

By no means all grandparents welcome these commitments. They want to see and spend time with their children and grandchildren, but would rather do so socially and when it suits them. Many speak sadly of having had to abandon retirement plans for leisure and travel. In a recent Australian study, some grandparents expressed open resentment at any assumption that they would take on the role of childcare provider for their grandchildren, and objected to this role being expected of them by their children or the community.

If I could say no without turning my daughter's work life upside down, and without losing my chance to see the children and her regularly, I would.

Maternal grandmother of three children

However, a grandparent who stands in for or backs up parents in caring for a child while the family is intact, especially if they have done so from babyhood, is likely to be highly placed in that child's 'attachment hierarchy'. Mother will come first and probably father next, but the third most important person in his life may well be a grandmother (or perhaps a grandfather), who will therefore be in an ideal position to help when the family breaks up.

Many grandfathers have moved into new roles with children just as their sons and sons-in-law have done. Many are, and are expected to be, interested in their grandchildren as well as loving, and their presence in the lives of father-deprived children can be invaluable. One grandfather, newly retired, expressed the sentiments of many when he said, 'When my children were growing up, I was so busy making a living I had very little time for them. Now my biggest joy is being with my grandchildren. Maybe I'm trying to make up for what I didn't do before.' However, although grandfathers, especially maternal grandfathers who have retired from work, often spend a lot of time with their grandchildren, even taking part in grandparent childcare, they almost always do it in partnership with their wives. Very few grandfathers take sole or even main responsibility for the care of a grandchild, whether he or she is being looked after at home or taken out for a treat.

RESEARCH

Grandfathers Caring for Grandchildren

When grandfathers reported looking after grandchildren, only 4 per cent of those interviewed said they took the main responsibility of care, while around half shared it with their partner or spouse and nearly half said their partner or spouse was solely responsible for the grandchildren. In contrast, more than half (54 per cent) of the grandmothers reported taking the main responsibility of care for grandchildren, with just over one-third saying they shared the responsibility with their partner or spouse.

Christine Millward, 'Family Relationship and Intergenerational Exchange in Later Life', Working paper no. 15, Australian Institute of Family Studies, Melbourne, 1998

Grandparents are not important only to babies and toddlers. A very large survey of childcare in the United Kingdom published in 2006 showed that almost one in five (19 per cent) of all families using any non-parental childcare for a child up to age five relied principally on care by a grandparent.

And grandparent care does not necessarily end even when children reach school age. In Australia in 2002, more children under the age of twelve received informal care by a grandparent than any other kind of care, formal or informal, while in 2006 The British Daycare Trust stated that each week a quarter of families with children under fifteen used a grandparent to look after a child for an average of sixteen hours per week, and many adolescents, who don't exactly need care and probably wouldn't be offered it from any other source, welcome grandparents' caring companionship when parents are not around.

In the holidays Gran and Gramps always say 'pop round if you need anything' and I do go round quite a lot. It's not exactly that I need anything – though Gran's a stellar cook – it's that hanging out with them makes a change from hanging out with my mates.

Boy, aged thirteen

The particular importance of grandparents to teenage grandchildren is highlighted in a study of communication in British families. During the survey period, more than one in five of the teenagers who had spent time with a grandparent while their parents were at work had talked to that grandparent about personal issues and problems, including family breakdown, a higher proportion than had discussed such things with parents, teachers or siblings.

Given the overwhelming importance of grandparents to many contemporary families, it is astonishing how little factual information we have about them. Even their identity is surrounded by question marks. It might seem that biology makes it perfectly clear who is and is not whose grandparent, but does it? If your child's grandmother is your husband's mother, she's your mother-in-law; if she's your mother, she's his mother-in-law, but what if she is his or your stepmother? One thing we do know is that not all grandparents are loved and loving, and if yours are not it is very likely due to family breakdown in an earlier generation.

QUOTES

Two Generations of Divorce

'Poor relationships between today's parents and grandparents are often planted in yesterday's anxieties and misunderstandings, predating the birth of the first grandchild. A divorce puts "ex" in front of most relationship names, and a remarriage introduces "step". Is the father of a parent's live-in lover her children's grandfather? And what about the new partner of the grandfather himself? Is she – or he – your children's step-grandmother or step-grandfather even if the role has not been formalised by law and the original partner is still around?'

Penelope Leach, *Childcare Today*, Vintage, 2010, p. 118

What we also know is that although research studies involving extended families do not always clearly distinguish between grandparents and other relatives, between maternal and paternal grandparents, or even between grandmothers and grandfathers, and while there are certainly aunts, cousins and step-everybody's who are lastingly important to children when immediate families break up, the relatives who are likely to matter most, in every country, are maternal grandmothers: mothers' biological or adoptive mothers, or very occasionally stepmothers.

Unfortunately, parental separation does not always bring grandparents closer to their children and grandchildren. Sometimes that special relationship shrivels in the cold blast of family breakdown, with less and less contact between grandparents and grandchildren, not only while a separation or divorce is underway but forever afterwards. Since it is the maternal grandmother, often supported by the maternal grandfather, who is most likely to be closely involved in supporting the separated family, and her support will be going to the mother and children, paternal grandparents are very vulnerable to gradual exclusion and fathers are likely to be left without much support from their own parents. In research surveys, parents mostly say that it is important for children to have as much contact with both sets of grandparents after their parents are separated or divorced as they did before, but in real life that doesn't often happen. Many parents cannot help seeing the two older-generation households as enemy camps and cannot tolerate the idea of older children confiding private details of one parent's life to the parents of the other.

> *I know they love him. And he loves them too. But taking him to see them is really hard for me because they've never really liked me, not from the first time their son took me to a movie. They didn't think I was good enough for him then, and now they're sure I'm not.*
>
> Mother of toddler, aged one and half years

EXTENDED FAMILY AND OTHER SPECIAL ADULTS

When parents are behaving oddly, it helps children of all ages to have other adults around whom they know and trust and who are still behaving normally. Different adults may be special to different children: one may hang on to a grandparent or caregiver; another may spend more and more time with the family of his best friend who lives close by, while it may be a teacher at school or college who is the most vital support for an older child or young adult.

Having your child strike up a close and confidential relationship with another adult – especially if it is not a family member – can leave you feeling hurt and anxious. Why will your child talk to that teacher when he absolutely refuses to talk to you? Why will your daughter take advice from a friend's mother but not from her own? Try to understand that those adults are more acceptable and useful to your child right now just because they are not you. With the family collapsing around him he is no longer sure what your values, judgements and viewpoints are, or whether he can go on assuming that what you do and say represents the adult world. He needs to find out whether other adults, especially adults he has sought out for himself, think and behave differently from you.

Most people that either of you tell about trouble in your family will inevitably take sides, of course. But if the two of you together confide in someone who is truly concerned for you all as a family, and is especially concerned for the children, he or she may provide you all with emotional ballast during the stormiest times. Be careful who you pick, though. Some people will make an enjoyable drama out of the sadness you are recounting, and enjoy passing it on, too. An obtuse or insensitive adult can rip scabs off children instead of putting sticking plaster on.

> *My mum's stepmother was really shocked when my mother left my father and moved in with another guy, a bit younger than her. I was about ten and I'd been told that they planned to marry and that my sisters and I could go and live with them. 'He may marry Emily,' said my grandmother, 'but there's no way he's going to take on you lot . . . Why would he?'*
>
> Man, now aged thirty

> *I was twelve and at boarding school, desperately miserable about what was going on at home, especially the brand new stepmother who'd arrived in Dad's house. The school matron caught me crying and I confided this to her. Do you know what she said? She said, 'You're really lucky to have two mothers.'*
>
> Woman, now aged fifty

It's not only your children who need support: as you and your partner tear yourselves apart you are both going to need other adults you can rely on. In theory every nuclear family is the nucleus of an extended family. In practise, though, in our individualistic society, a nuclear family is often a more or less stand-alone unit consisting only of a couple in a sexual partnership and children for whom they are solely responsible.

Nuclear families are all very well as long as all's well, but if there is nothing and nobody to support them from outside they are horribly vulnerable to disintegration if that central couple relationship goes wrong. It's when that's happening that the importance of extended family – or any other kind of support from outside – becomes painfully clear.

> Her mum, dad, two aunts and an uncle lived three doors down from us. I'd sometimes felt they were a bit too much in our faces, if you know what I mean, but when I moved out and moved away I realised just how important they were, and to me as well as to her.
>
> Her dad and her uncle were the people I went to the pub with. That held me together during the worst months before we separated, and not having that was one of the loneliest bits of living on my own. To my ex and the kids, their house was an extension of ours. I think it was the popping in and out that held her together, plus any or all of the women took care of Mandy so she had time to herself. Without it, she says, Mandy would have had a pretty boring six months and seen and heard a lot of crying and screaming. Kate liked to go and join in after school. She specially loved one of the aunties who had lots of laughs for her at a time when her mum really didn't. And Jenny: well, being a bit older, I suppose, she worried about her mum and about me and about what was going to happen, and she took all that to her gran . . .
>
> Father of three daughters, aged two, six and eight

PARENTS' LOVERS AND POTENTIAL PARTNERS

Parents separate for 'grown-up' reasons, and often because one or both of them want a new and different 'grown-up' life. Sometimes those reasons are clear fault-lines in the original marriage, such as one or both partners being abusive, alcoholic or perhaps addicted to drugs or gambling. But often those 'grown-up' reasons are to do with having found, or being on the lookout for, a new sexual partnership.

If your marriage is falling apart primarily over an affair with another man or woman, children will soon know, and if they are old enough to think about other people's relationships at all – over seven, say – will probably see the stranger as having stolen one parent from the other. There is a childish parallel in shifting best-friendships at school, and children may find such a 'theft' a more comprehensible – and even forgivable – reason for parents separating than the incomprehensible emotional betrayal of just not loving each other any more. But if children usually forgive the 'stolen' parent-as-victim, they may not easily forgive the person who 'stole' him or her. If the love affair turns out to be a life affair, this can be a nightmarish route into step-parenting.

If another person comes on your scene after you have separated and new living arrangements have been achieved, do your ex the courtesy of telling him or her before anyone else does. Don't be in a hurry to tell your children, though, or to introduce him or her to them. They may deeply resent anyone who even looks like edging into a missing parent's place, but that's the less dire of two equally probable possibilities. Far from resenting a new person, children who have recently lost their taken-for-granted-everyday father (or mother) are often easily enraptured by the making-an-effort charms of a new candidate. If a New Man plays football in the garden with the middle one, shoulders the littlest one on walks, talks usefully to the oldest about her forthcoming exam and makes you laugh, he may soon be a welcome visitor and within weeks an important part of the children's lives. If the two of you then decide that the relationship is not going anywhere – and face it, not many affairs do – childish hearts will be broken all over again. Not because losing this lover-man is as bad as losing their dad, but because losing their dad has left them acutely vulnerable to loss and the household short of an adult male. Although children react differently to changes to a household they visit rather than live in, roughly the same possibilities apply if the children's father introduces a new lover.

What little research there is strongly suggests that it's best to keep the new person merely as one of your friends in the children's eyes. Try not to let them sense that the relationship is special and any business of theirs until you are truly convinced that it is going to be long-lasting and a partnership is planned between you and ready for implementation.

Until that time comes (if it ever does):

- Don't have a new sexual partner staying overnight with you when the children are in the house. Their reaction to finding you in bed or in the shower together will vary according to their ages, but every variation will be disastrous.
- Don't underestimate children's ability to pick up clues to this 'friendship' being special. It doesn't take finding an intimate garment in the laundry basket to raise a child's suspicions; switching to the brand of tea he or she prefers or changing the newspaper you take may be enough.
- If the children live with you, don't encourage – or even allow – a new lover the privilege of parent-like behaviour with your children, however tempting it may be to enlist his or her skills in making a birthday cake, picking up your daughter from a late party or backing up your discipline.
- If the children live with your ex, don't try to squeeze in extra time with your lover by joining him or her into the time you spend with your children. When they come to visit, they want to see you and only you, and they want to see you as you are with them, not as you are with your new partner.
- Try not to change access arrangements simply in order to give

yourself more child-free time to spend with this new person. If you didn't think it was a good idea for your two-year-old to sleep over with her father at weekends a month ago, it almost certainly isn't a good idea now, just because you want your lover to sleep over with you.

If and when you are seriously contemplating making this relationship a partnership:

- If you want to try out the business of living together as a potential family group, try and do it on neutral territory rather than by inviting him or her to come and live with you and the children. If the money and the time can be afforded, a rented holiday home is often a good start. Nobody's territory is being invaded; nobody knows how to manage this environment so everyone can work out the ground-rules for living in it together.

- Make sure your potential new partner realises that your children already have two parents (even if they only see one at a time) and don't need any more. Sometimes well-meaning people assume that lone parents want help with their parenting when what they really want help with is the lone bit. Make it clear that if all goes well, he or she can eventually become a highly significant adult in your children's lives but never their parent.

- Beware of authority. Few children will readily accept instructions or reproofs from a comparative stranger, but many adults find it difficult to live with children without giving any. If your potential partner cannot manage this now, it is very likely to become a problem if you marry.

- Beware of manipulation. Many children work hard to influence parents' choice of partner, usually in the direction of getting rid of them. Techniques vary from the blatant (spiders in shoes) to the more subtle (pretend she isn't there at all). Either can be most successfully off-putting.

- Be sure it is understood that whatever the issue, you are and must be a parent first before you are a partner, and that as a parent you will be communicating with your ex and doing your best to maintain a cooperative – or at least polite – relationship.

CHILDREN'S STEP-PARENTS

Even if your child has known the soon-to-be step-parent for many months and really likes him or her, you may find that once he knows you are planning an actual marriage or permanent live-in partnership his attitude changes for the worse.

> I was twelve when they finally decided they wanted to get married and I realised I was going to have a stepfather. I don't know what got into me but I told a pack of made-up lies about him to my school friends – stupid things like he wore sandals with socks, which he never did – and to my gran. I even told Gran I didn't want to live with him and could I come and live with her. It's lucky I didn't make things up and tell them to my dad or it might really have caused trouble. But why did I tell my best friend I hated the man my mum was going to marry? I liked him a lot and I'd known him for nearly two years as our closest family friend . . .
>
> Girl, now aged sixteen

Children can develop extremely close and warm relationships with step-parents. Some even maintain that, despite the misery they felt at the time, they are glad now that there was a divorce.

> I'm closer to my stepdad than I've ever been or ever would have been to my real father. I just like him better. I think he's a much nicer man. And he makes my mum laugh. As to my littlest

sister, she's three now and I think she really feels like he's Daddy. She doesn't call him Daddy 'cause Mum says things like 'you've got one of those already', but she calls him 'my-Da' in a soppy sort of a voice. Mum thought I might mind but I don't.

Boy, aged twelve

However, most children whose parents have divorced are not at all glad to have a step-parent. Many have found it impossible to accept that their parents' separation is permanent, and they often go on for years after the divorce has been finalised dreaming of a reconciliation. Even for an older child who really knows that a dream is only a dream and isn't going to happen, the idea of a parent marrying for a second time and finally moving those dream goalposts from improbable to impossible is difficult to cope with.

Helping your children to accept the prospect and reality of a step-parent

- Although children survive the trauma of parental separation better if other aspects of life can stay the same, the positive step of making a new family grouping usually works more easily in a new environment. In these circumstances, a house-move often makes a better start than having all of you move in with him (or her) or vice versa. In a new home, everyone shares mutual territory about which nobody feels possessive, and there can be mutual ground-rules for living in it from the beginning.
- Leaving room for the 'real' parent is vital. That means room in the child's life – so that his regular visiting days and weekends don't suddenly get lost in new-family activities – and psychological room, too. Don't expect a child to call the step-parent 'Mum' or 'Dad', for example (unless he asks, or does it spontaneously), or press him to make a Mother's Day card for the stepmother instead of, or even as well as, his actual mother.

- Try to make the new relationship completely extra to, rather than instead of, the original one. And make sure room is left for the old family, too. Encourage children's relationships with your ex's family.
- Although their relationship is because of you, the step-parent and children cannot make it through you. Try not to stand in the middle, like a maypole around which everybody dances. Step-parents and children need to get to know one another as people rather than as your appendages.
- Don't expect the step-parent or children to accept sex-stereotyped family roles too quickly (if at all). A stepfather, for example, usually needs to go very easily on 'discipline', 'manners' and so forth. With adolescents he may never be permitted an authoritative relationship, but may, if he will accept it, eventually be offered friendship instead. A stepmother will probably need to hold back on personal care, however warmly she feels towards the children. Trying to plait hair or wash necks will be seen as 'stepping beyond the bounds', at least until the children spontaneously hug and kiss her.
- Try to arrange for the step- and natural parent to meet, especially if you have managed to keep your relationship civil since the divorce. Children need to feel that all the adults who are closely concerned with them are on the same side: their side. It also helps if they do not feel that they can at all easily play one off against the other or have their wilder fantasies believed.

CHAPTER 4

PRACTICAL AND LEGAL ISSUES

The change from having both parents living with them in the same home to having the two of you living in separate places is one of the biggest a child can ever face. You cannot avoid that change, but as you struggle with the sadness and the guilt of parental separation, you may find it comforting and helpful to realise what a lot of practical aspects of your children's new lives you can control, and how much that can do to protect or rebuild their happiness and wellbeing.

Parental separation tends to bring other changes along with it, such as moving to a new home, changing from one caregiver or nursery to another, or going to a new school. These are normal life-events which most children find highly stressful even if they are securely embedded in intact families, but which can be not just stressful but devastating when they are part of the abnormal disruption of the family caused by parental separation. When family is in turmoil, the more smoothly the rest of their lives can carry on as before, the better children will cope. So before you plan on – or just accept – big changes like the ones dealt with in this chapter, make sure you ask yourselves – and each other – about other options. Above all, think geography.

FAMILY GEOGRAPHY AND CHILDREN'S SECURITY

Children's security depends on the people to whom they are attached being available. When parents separate, children lose the security of being able to take the presence of both of them together or either one of them at a time for granted. That's a huge loss, but just how acute and lasting it is largely depends on everybody's proximity. Daddy has left and that's awful, but where has he gone? The answer 'into a flat in the next road' is less awful than 'the other side of town' and very, very much less awful than 'a three-hour journey away', not to mention 'to Australia' or, worst of all, 'don't know'. Everything that is most important and most difficult about making a separated family work for children depends primarily on parents maintaining a reasonable relationship with each other, and staying within easy geographical reach of each other comes a close second.

Avoiding the other big, stressful changes in children's lifestyle that will make parental separation harder to bear is also largely a matter of geography. If after one parent leaves, the other could find a way of staying in the same home, the children could keep the bedrooms and the play space they are used to; keep the family cat or the beloved rabbits; stay in the same schools; and keep their whole network of friends and neighbours – and so could you. Even if staying in the same house is financially impossible, a smaller, cheaper home in the same neighbourhood would still let them keep the familiar infrastructure of their lives.

THE NEED FOR A HOME BASE

However many places there are where he spends time, a child must live somewhere, must have a home. A place and setting that we think of as 'home' is highly important to most humans but it may be especially so to children because they have so little control over their own lives and lack adults' nest-making experience and skills. If you move, temporarily or permanently, you will know where you are going – even if you go reluctantly – and whether it is into a new flat, a hotel room or a prison cell, you will at once settle down to making the new place feel as homelike as you can. A child who is moved has no idea where he is going or what it will be like. If the new place is stable and somebody helps him settle in it, he will eventually get past the fact that it is not home so that it can become so and give him back his security. But until or unless he has a home base, his life will lack stability.

Almost all children do move house; on average, families in the UK and the USA move four to six times while children are growing up. But most house-moves are job-related, are chosen (or at least accepted) by the parents, and maintain or even upgrade the family's standard of living. A house-move resulting from a family break-up is different; it is not something that both parents have chosen – indeed, the loss of one parent is implicit in it, and as if that huge change in the family's lifestyle was not painful enough, the new place will usually be a step down. The contrast experienced by the eleven-year-old quoted below when she was moved from isolated countryside to inner-city living was extreme, but the devastation she experienced is relevant to many families, because if her parents had looked at the move more from her point of view they might have managed to make it less lastingly traumatic.

It wasn't just moving house; it was moving life. We'd lived deep in the country ever since I could remember (actually since I was three). I'd had a pony since I was seven. She was the centre of everything I did and most of what I thought, too. Leaving her behind just felt like everything had come to an end. Like I had come to an end. And I didn't understand how to be in London. How could you play in a little garden with people either side

and rows of windows looking at you? Was I angry with them?
No. I was too sad, too bewildered to be angry. I think I was
grown up and a parent myself before I could feel properly
furious.

Adult woman, looking back to when she was eleven

Do arrange for the children and whichever parent is to live with them to stay in their existing home if that is at all possible, at least during the upheaval of the actual separation. They will get used to a home with only one parent in it a great deal more easily if the home is home. Changes within that home will probably be less disturbing than a move. A (carefully selected) lodger, for example, might bring a mortgage within reach without bothering children nearly as much as leaving the house. Be careful about doubling the children up so as to free a bedroom to rent out, though. Once children have had a bedroom each, those separate rooms often become exceedingly important – perhaps especially to teenagers – and being suddenly forced to share can jeopardise sibling relationships just when they are at their most important.

If staying in the same home is impractical, try to look at the move from the children's points of view as far as practicalities allow. You may not be able to achieve what they want, but if you don't think about what it is that they want, you cannot even try. A manageable journey to the same school and friendship group may be more important to your ten- to sixteen-year-old than any feature of the new home itself, while to younger children features of the new place, such as a garden or some outside play space, may be crucial, and anywhere that could not include the family cat or dog might be a disastrously poor choice.

Living in two places at once

If the two of you share the care of your children after separation you may each want your place to be the one they think of as 'home'.

Do be careful not to let that become one more of the many issues which your children feel they cannot even talk about for fear of hurting one of their parent's feelings. Squabbling over which place is home can make them feel that neither is, and that is a pity because children need to live 'at home', however much time they spend somewhere else.

For children under four or five, 'home' will almost certainly be the place where Mum lives. If your children are past that stage and one of you lives in the ex-family home or has a much more child-friendly place than the other, the question of which is 'home' will settle itself. Likewise, if the children live almost full time with whichever of you is resident parent (or 'parent with care'), it's unlikely that the place where they visit the other parent – perhaps overnight at weekends – will be labelled 'home'. However, if both of you are fortunate enough to have places to live that the children like, especially if they are in the same neighbourhood so that school and friends are accessible from either, and the two of you are in civil contact with each other, you may find that older children eventually come to regard both places in a similar way and the term 'home' is dropped in favour of 'Dad's' and 'Mum's'.

Even under those relatively idyllic circumstances, though, it isn't easy for a child to feel equally at home in two places. An adolescent might (theoretically at least) be able to decide spontaneously which home he's heading for on any particular day. If he decides to go to Dad's (because he'd like them to watch the cricket together), all he has to do is call his mum to say he won't be there today, and his dad to say he will; then he should be good to go, able to let himself in and assured that he'll find everything he needs where he left it. In the real world, though, people usually have to make plans and arrangements, if only so that somebody buys supper and gets it eaten and nobody buys supper and gets it wasted.

Whether you are trying to help your children feel that they have two homes as well as two parents, or arranging for smooth and enjoyable visits from your home to the other parent's, it helps to keep the business of transferring from one to the other as simple as possible – though that may not be very simple.

- Cut down the amount of clobber they need to think about, pack up and carry backwards and forwards with them in order to be comfortable in either house. PJs, washing things, hairdryer/ tongs and an alarm clock can easily be duplicated. Clothes are more difficult. In the holidays, younger children may be fine for weekends as long as they have underwear and socks, a pair of trainers, a set of old clothes to mess around in, swimming gear and a waterproof and wellies. If it's school tomorrow, they'll need clean uniforms. And keep checking everything for size . . .

> *Why do my boots shrink when they stay at Daddy's house?*
>
> Girl, aged three

- Clothing in two places for teenagers is much more difficult. They want to wear the clothes they want to wear, not the clothes that happen to be available, so the current selection will always have to go from one place to another.
- There are affordable ways of duplicating electronic equipment they can't do without. Instead of each older child needing his laptop, for instance, make sure you have the software they use for school work and socialising on your computer, and encourage them to carry stuff backwards and forwards on a stick.
- Many visits are ruined by lack of the right charger or cut short by leaving medical essentials behind. Make sure they can charge phones and tablets (and whatever else they have) in either place and that regular medicines and emergency-use items such as inhalers are duplicated.
- Don't feel that you have to try and make both places as like each other as possible. A four- or five-year-old may settle more easily

if his bedding is familiar and the nightlight is 'right', but as long as even slightly older children feel secure in the place they think of as 'home' and are able to leave it and the resident parent easily, the fact that the other parent's place is different can be part of the pleasure of regular visits, in addition to the pleasure of spending time with him. Differences between the two homes can be part of the fun, giving children a bit of space in which to be different people. Different food, different music, different conversation, different games and different ground-rules can all be interesting extensions of life in home-base.

SCHOOLS

Sometimes parents forget how important school is to a child. Don't lose sight of it. While the routines of going to school, the school's hours, the breaks and the holiday dates are an important part of the structure of family life (and will lend children stability during the upheavals of parental separation), what actually goes on in school can strike parents as a mixture of mystery and trivia and something they don't have to think much about. Parents who are very taken up with trying to work out how to manage a separation are especially likely to take school for granted and think about the home-child they see and know as if that was the whole child. It is not the whole child, of course.

Folk-wisdom says that 'school days are the happiest days of your life'. It's sad to think of a whole adult life offering no greater happiness than being a school child, but if school days are not at least moderately and mostly happy, your child will be unhappy overall. He has got to spend most of the waking hours of around 245 days of each year in school. It is not just a place where he goes to learn while his 'real life' carries on at home. It is the place where he will have (or not have) most of his friends; where he will make (or not make) most of his meaningful relationships with non-family adults; where he will find (or fail to find) most of his sporting and leisure activities. School will and should be central to his life, so no parent is entitled to ignore what goes on there.

Getting support from school

School may be especially important to children when parents are separating, because when things are in a muddle at home, school can provide much-needed structure and predictability, and being with peers may be a welcome distraction. If your very young child is liable to be tearful and visibly upset at school, it may be help-ful to tell her teacher what is going on at home – or at least that something is – so that she can keep a sympathetic eye on her. An older child may not want anyone to know about your separation and you should respect his or her confidence if you can. But if teachers express surprise because a previously cooperative student is being difficult, even aggressive, it is obviously better that they should know that he is under particular stresses, so that any complaints about his behaviour are dealt with as sympathetically as possible.

Sometimes it is not your child's behaviour at school that causes anxiety but difficulty in getting him to school. Acute anxiety over going to school may be triggered by something that happened to you, not to him, and made him wonder if you were 'all right'. Sometimes the trigger is an obviously traumatic one, such as par-ents' actually separating, but sometimes it is something more trivial. Seeing you in tears, perhaps, which made the child aware that you were unhappy, or an overheard row between you and his father, which made him wonder whether all was well between you or whether his family was going to break up.

Once a child is sensitive to your welfare and feels that he has to keep an eye out to be sure you are 'all right', being away at school all day can become intolerable because he imagines all the fearful things that may have happened to you while he was gone.

Do go immediately to see whichever teacher is most concerned with your child's wellbeing and enlist the school's help for him. Meanwhile, make sure that the child understands what is going on between you and his other parent, what is going to happen and what you feel about it. The reality is sad but it is nowhere near as terrifying as those fantasies. Between your efforts and those of a sympathetic teacher he may be able to cope, but if someone else to talk to would make it easier, you may be able to enlist further help from a counsellor employed by the school.

Changing schools

Going to a new school is a big and important change for most children. Regular moves as children get older are built in to the school systems of different countries, with the big UK moves being into school 'reception' at four or five, from primary to secondary school at eleven, and from secondary school to sixth form or college at sixteen. Those regular moves are recognised as stressful for children, not only because new institutions with their different organisational structures and demands are always daunting, but also because leaving the school a child is settled in always involves losing some important relationships, which have to be replaced in the new one.

Children who move at the expected 'transition' times and within the same community will usually find themselves moving up the system with at least some classmates and into a school that knows where they have come from and has probably put a lot of thought into its 'transition arrangements'. The children who are likely to find the move really difficult are the ones who move from one school to another outside those expected times, especially if they move mid-year and perhaps to a different area of the country.

Part of the importance of the relationships children make in school and the activities they take up is that they are separate from you and from home. You cannot do it for him (as you may have done in nursery or pre-school), but you may be able to help him do it for himself. Whatever the age of the child, there is always a fine line to be drawn between interference and neglect in a parent's dealings with a school. The happy medium has something to do with always being interested enough to listen, and a lot to do with always being willing, even eager, to be involved whenever the child or the school issues any kind of invitation. When your child is starting at a school where he knows nobody and is the only one who is new, a bit of extra parental participation will certainly help, but what will help most of all is your awareness of what he is up against and your ability to sense when he is struggling and wants your support, and when he is managing himself and wants to live his school life without any parental involvement at all.

As well as being immediately stressful for children, extra and ill-timed school moves may also reduce school performance. Figures from the Royal Society of Arts think-tank shows that children who change schools outside the traditional first years of primary and secondary education in England do worse in exams than peers who do not; the decline in attainment increases with each change of school.

RESEARCH

Between the Cracks

Each year, 300,000 children move schools. Children from families eligible for free school meals – with a household income of less than £25,000 a year, at the time of writing – make up about 40 per cent of the total, well above the 26 per cent of pupils who receive free meals nationally.

However, poverty and disadvantage does not fully explain the ill-effects of these school moves:

'Even after adjusting for prior attainment and social background, we're confident that there is a negative impact happening to these people because of in-year moves.'

Report from the Royal Society of Arts Education
Think-tank, 2013

MONEY MATTERS

Your ability to keep the practical aspects of family life running smoothly while the emotional part is struggling will unfortunately depend largely on money.

Don't underestimate the costs of getting a divorce in the first place. In the UK a reasonably cooperative divorce will cost around £1,300, which is about 3 per cent of the annual salary of a well-to-do family and as much as 9 per cent of the least well-paid. If the two of you cannot work out the terms of your divorce between you, so that solicitors have to be enlisted, the costs of your divorce will soar and so will its emotional costs to your children. The more you fight the more you will pay and they will suffer.

As we have seen (see Introduction), people who are well-off are less likely to get divorced in the first place, but if they do split up, a good income certainly helps to pad everybody's wounds. However comfortably off you may be when your separation becomes inevitable, though, it is likely that you will be very much poorer by the time things settle down.

- The resources that have supported one home and family will have to support two.
- Some expensive possessions may have to be doubled up – the car, for instance.
- Resources may dwindle if, for example, it is impossible for both of you to go on working full time because childcare arrangements

that formerly made it possible (such as a nanny or a full-time nursery place) are no longer affordable.

- If you and the children move out of the neighbourhood, childcare help that was available without cost from grandparents or friends may be out of geographical reach.
- If the other parent moves out of the district, staying in contact with the children will depend on there being money for travel.

FACTS

Single-Parent Families and Poverty in the UK, 2013

- Children in single-parent families have a much higher risk of living in poverty than children in couple families. At the time of writing, around four in every ten (41 per cent) children in single-parent families are poor, compared to just over two in every ten children in couple families.
- Paid work is not a guaranteed route out of poverty for single parents; the poverty rate for single-parent families where the parent works part time is 23 per cent; where the parent works full time it is 18 per cent.
- The median weekly income of working single-parent families doing sixteen hours a week or more is £337, compared with £491 for couple families with one worker and £700 where both parents work.
- Of working single parents who are paying for childcare, 32 per cent, as compared with 22 per cent of couples where one partner is in work, find it difficult to meet those costs. Thirty-four per cent had a childcare arrangement with the child's grandparent; 17 per cent had an arrangement with their ex-partner.
- Forty-three per cent of single parents are social housing tenants compared to 12 per cent of couples.

- Of all single-parent renters, 71 per cent were eligible for UK housing benefit in 2011 compared to 25 per cent of all couple renters.
- Single-parent households are the most likely to be in arrears on one or more household bills, mortgage or non-mortgage borrowing commitment (31 per cent).
- Thirty-eight per cent of single parents said that money always runs out before the end of the week/month compared to 19 per cent of couples.
- Sixty-three per cent of single parents have no savings compared to 34 per cent of couples.

The Facts About Single Parents, Gingerbread.org.UK/
Statistics, 2013

Although the challenges facing poor single parents are enormous, recent studies on both sides of the Atlantic show that many one-parent families adopt highly adaptive parenting and lifestyles, promoting education, resourcefulness and responsibility in their children.

Child maintenance

Child maintenance in the UK – financial support that helps towards a child's everyday living costs – is for children under six-teen or under twenty for those in full-time education. It is paid by the parent who doesn't have day-to-day care of the child (the 'paying parent') to the parent or person such as a grandparent or guardian who does (the 'receiving parent'). There are statutory services (the Child Support Agency or CSA and the Child Maintenance Service), which will work out how much ought to be paid in your particular circumstances and will, in theory at least, collect it for you.

Changes were made in the UK child support system in 2012 to encourage more couples to make their own arrangements. Many of those who continue to seek help from the statutory bodies have to pay towards the service.

FACTS

Types of Help Available from Statutory Child Maintenance Services (UK and USA)

These services can help you to:

- find the other parent if you do not have an address;
- sort out any issues concerning parentage, arranging DNA testing if necessary (https://www.gov.uk/ arranging-child-maintenance-child-support-agency/ disagreements-about-parentage);
- work out how much child maintenance should be paid (https://www.gov.uk/how-child-maintenance-is-worked-out);
- arrange for the 'paying parent' to pay child maintenance;
- pass payments on to the 'receiving parent';
- look at the payments again when either parent reports changes in their circumstances (https://www.gov.uk/ arranging-child-maintenance-child-support-agency/ changes-you-need-to-report);
- take action if payments are not made, including having the employer withhold money from the parent's pay-packet or benefits (https://www.gov.uk/arranging-child-maintenance-child-support-agency/nonpayment-what-happens; http://www.acf.hhs.gov/programs/css).

Unfortunately, these services are not always as good as they sound. Don't overestimate this source of financial help with caring for your children after you have separated from their other parent. The system is overburdened and unwieldy, so despite the large range and draconian nature of the measures available to enforce payments, less than 40 per cent of single parents in the UK receive any maintenance from their child's other parent, and those who do, whether through the CSA or by private arrangement, receive an average weekly amount of only around £45 per family (not per child). Of single parents receiving child maintenance exclusively through the CSA, 40 per cent receive less than £10 per week, 38 per cent receive between £10 and £50 per week, and 22 per cent receive more than £50 per week.

When resident parents receive less maintenance than they should, it is not always because their ex-partners refuse to pay what they owe or because agencies fail to take action to ensure payment. Sometimes it is because the agency's original calculations of what should be paid were incorrect. There are many unfortunate fathers who, having made regular payments of exactly what they were told they owed, suddenly hear that the level of payment was inadequate from the beginning and they now face accumulated arrears. To avoid this it is probably wise to check the claim made on you for child maintenance using one of several do-it-yourself calculators available on the internet. If the claim seems low, don't gratefully assume that it is correct: query it with the agency or your solicitor.

Some parents are surprised to discover that child maintenance and access are not legally connected. Fathers often feel that paying maintenance gives them the right to see the children, when in fact the children have a right to see their fathers whether they pay maintenance or not. Likewise, many mothers whose exes do not pay the maintenance that is due from them are taken aback when they find that they cannot legally use non-payment as a reason to deny or limit fathers' access, or use the threat of denying access to force them to pay. The vital point for both parents to remember is that children are the subjects rather than the objects of both maintenance money and access visits. The money is not paid by the father to the mother for her benefit but for the child's. And access visits are not a father's privilege which he must earn, or can lose, but a child's right.

LEGAL ISSUES

In order to embark on divorcing, or dissolving a civil partnership, you have to apply to the family court for permission, fill in a divorce petition form and pay a court fee, £550 at the time of writing. You must show your reasons for wanting to end the marriage. These may include adultery, unreasonable behaviour (such as domestic violence, drug-taking or refusal to pay for housekeeping), desertion, having lived apart for more than two years and both agreeing to the divorce. If the divorce is 'undefended' – that is, your soon-to-be-ex-partner accepts it – and the court accepts your reasons, you will receive a 'decree nisi' (a 'no-reason-why-not' document) and, six weeks later, the marriage will be legally ended with a 'decree absolute'.

Defended divorces, in which one partner seeks divorce and the other resists it, are unusual. The person seeking the divorce has to convince the court that the marriage has irretrievably broken down for any of the above reasons, despite anything the other partner may say. If the couple have lived apart for five years rather than for two, irretrievable breakdown will be taken for granted. Otherwise the plaintiff has to convince the court. It is very rare for the court to refuse permission to petition for divorce, but it can happen, especially if the reason given is 'unreasonable behaviour' and the behaviour cited is difficult to prove – such as 'insensitivity' or 'emotional bullying' – and the court must judge which party to believe.

A divorce petition that is not defended, and working out the terms of your divorce between you, will save a great deal of stress, time and, above all, money. Don't expect financial assistance – even if divorced friends have told you about legal aid – because it will probably not be forthcoming. In the UK the government has cut legal aid for much of family law as part of spending reductions, and divorce is now only eligible for legal aid if it is being sought because of child protection issues or proven domestic violence.

FACTS

Changes to Legal Aid in the UK

Until April 2013 people who were eligible for legal aid (see below) could receive its assistance to cover all aspects of family law, including divorce, disputes between unmarried partners and the dissolution of civil partnerships, financial disputes, property disputes and disputes over arrangements for children.

Now, following the Legal Aid, Sentencing and Punishment of Offenders Act (LASPO) of 2012, legal aid for those private family law problems is available only to individuals who can produce evidence of domestic abuse or the risk of it, or where there are child protection issues.

If you are eligible for legal aid you will receive it only in matters of:

- public family law regarding child protection (i.e. care proceedings);
- private family law where there is evidence of child abuse;
- child abduction or the threat of it;
- representation of children in private family cases;
- forced marriage protection orders;
- legal advice in support of mediation;
- domestic violence injunction cases.

> ### *Changes to Eligibility and to the Scope of Legal Aid*
> Qualifications for legal aid have changed.
>
> Previously, receipt of a passporting benefit – income support; income-related support and employment allowance; income-based jobseeker's allowance; guarantee credit part of pension credit; universal credit – automatically rendered the individual eligible. Now an assessment of capital is also made and the size of the recipient's contributions has been increased.

Seeking mediation

If you are both willing to try to come to an agreement, but find it impossible to make plans together that will really stick, mediation may help. Mediation is not legal advice (although a court may instruct you to seek it), and it is not counselling; it is designed to help people sort out their differences for themselves and reach genuine agreement. Mediation will not focus on resolving emotional issues or relationship breakdown, but on practical matters. The mediator, who will neither take sides nor tell you what to do, meets with the two of you, usually for several weekly sessions, and encourages you to set out your disagreements openly and honestly, and to resolve them yourselves. Mediation seldom works unless both of you genuinely want to reach agreement; but provided you do want to, it is often effective, even if your views were poles apart at the beginning. Mediation is not free, but it is usually considerably less expensive than taking legal advice and in some cases legal aid will be available to contribute to the fees. Make sure you ask about costs before you begin.

Negotiating through a solicitor

If an impartial mediator cannot help you to reach joint decisions about getting divorced or about the terms, especially if you feel that you are being bullied or threatened towards an 'agreement' you don't want to accept, you may need a solicitor to help you negotiate, and if one of you has a solicitor, the other parent will need to have their own. Choose carefully though, especially with the wellbeing of your children in mind. Some people report that the involvement of legal professionals and the courts contributed more to chaos than to calm in children's lives. Certainly the adversarial system solicitors represent and work within can make for an atmosphere of unrelenting hostility, even aggression, between separating parents, so that even if you are trying to cooperate for the children's good, involvement of legal professionals makes it more difficult. When it comes to children's living arrangements and to access for a non-resident parent, you may seem to be the only people paying attention to what will work for younger children or being prepared to listen to what older children want.

In order to reduce the adversarial atmosphere that tends to surround these negotiations, a growing minority of solicitors are practising what is often referred to as 'collaborative law' in which you and your ex-partner meet and discuss your differences face to face, as you might do in mediation, but with the important difference that each of you has your own solicitor present at each meeting. Unlike a mediator, each solicitor will provide his or her client with support and advice, but unlike traditional practice in which solicitors work against each other, they will work together in the interests of helping the two of you reach mutual agreements.

When you have met with a solicitor you find sympathetic, make sure you understand the likely costs before you ask him or her to act on your behalf. Some solicitors (including some practising collaborative law) offer 'fixed fee family law services' in which the costs of each stage of your case are laid down in advance. This makes it very much easier to budget. Without such an arrangement, costs that accumulate outside meetings – for phone calls, for example, or for photocopying and posting documents to your ex's solicitor – can be unexpected and surprisingly high. Unlike a mediator, a solicitor who is not practising collaborative law will be on the side of the person who employs him or her (which is why each of you may want to employ your own). It is the individual who sought the consultation and will pay the bill whose rights and options will be addressed. When you have decided which of these options you want to pursue, your solicitor will negotiate on your behalf with your ex's solicitor.

Whether you and your ex-partner iron out your disagreements between yourselves or with the help of a mediator or a solicitor, your agreement will only be legally binding once you have obtained a 'consent order'. Drafted by a solicitor and signed in draft by both of you, a 'consent order' is a legally binding document that confirms your detailed agreement concerning financial affairs, property and child maintenance. Do make sure that your consent order is ratified by the court. There have been cases in which agreements were left in draft, leaving them open to being re-addressed by one of the parties who, sometimes years later, saw a possibility of improving his or her settlement.

If negotiation fails

If you and your ex cannot agree on arrangements for your children, you may have to apply to the court to decide between you on the outstanding matters.

Before making application to the court you should contact a mediator, because since the passage of the Children and Families Act 2014 parents will not be given permission to apply to the family court to resolve financial issues or arrangements for children until or unless they have attended a Mediation Information and Assessment Meeting, known as a MIAM. If you are eligible for legal aid it will be available to help you pay for legal advice on finding a mediator and to help you pay for family mediation.

The above bill also sets out a clear statement of courts' presumption that when parents separate it is in any child's best interests to have both parents involved in his or her life unless the contrary is shown. This is intended to reduce the possibility of one parent using court proceedings to punish or exclude the other.

That presumption does not hold if there are issues around child protection or domestic violence. However, a case showing that involvement with both parents is not in the child's interests cannot be made on the basis of one parent's fears or suspicions of the other. A parent who wishes to bring such a case to court – with or without any legal aid for which, under these exceptional circumstances, he or she might be eligible – will have to supply evidence of being a victim of domestic violence or that child abuse has taken place, and that she or he is divorcing or separating from an abusive partner.

Asking the court to decide

You should be aware that taking your divorce disputes to court is a last resort and in no way an easy option. Without access to legal aid you may find it impossible to afford legal representation and may have to represent yourself.

You can apply for a single court order, or a number of them, depending on which issues remain outstanding between the two of you. The court will make a particular order if – and only if – it considers that it would be best for the child, and this is usually the case. Bear in mind, though, that the order you get may not be the order you hoped for but the one the court considers in the child's best interests.

A child's mother, father or anyone with parental responsibility can apply for a court order. Other people, such as grandparents, can also apply but must first get permission from the court.

Making an application to the court

Whoever is making the application to the court must complete a form stating the reason for the application and pay a fee. The court will set a date for the application to be heard and may ask CAFCASS (Children and Family Court Advisory and Support Service) – the independent organisation which looks after the interests of children in family proceedings – for its input. If CAFCASS is involved it should send you information about its role and the court process. CAFCASS will try to speak to you and the other parent before the court hearing to find out more about the situation, and may also contact your local council and other services such as the police to see if they hold any information that might show safety or welfare concerns about your children. CAFCASS will write to the court before the first hearing telling them about the work they have done and advising the court on what it considers to be in the children's best interests.

The first hearing

Usually, parents, any legal advisers, an officer from CAFCASS (in Wales, CAFCASS officers are called family court advisers) and a district judge will attend the first hearing. Any particular problems will be discussed and the judge will try to reach a quick on-the-spot agreement where possible. If an agreement is reached at the first hearing, the court can decide whether or not to make an order confirming arrangements.

After the first hearing

If an agreement has not been reached at the first hearing, the court may require you and the non-resident parent to attend a meeting about mediation, or a separated parents' information programme.

The court may decide to arrange another hearing for a later date, allowing time for more evidence to be gathered and a CAFCASS report prepared, which will include talking to your children, if they are considered old enough, about their wishes and feelings. If the case is very complex the judge may ask for an assessment of the family dynamics and the children's relationships with each parent by an Expert Witness.

The family court can make many different orders and these can go into an astonishing amount of detail. The orders that are most commonly applied for used to be called 'residence orders' and 'contact orders'. They are now part of a group called child arrangements orders.

- A child arrangements order replacing a residence order sets out where and with whom a child should live.
- A child arrangements order replacing a contact order lays down the amount of contact the non-resident parent should have with the child; how contact should be made; and, if necessary, where this contact should take place. If a court, social worker or solicitor decides that the non-resident parent might harm either the child or the resident parent during ordinary contact, or might seek to kidnap the child, an order may be made for the non-resident parent to meet with the child only in the neutral environment of a contact centre.

As well as parents or guardians, partners in a marriage or civil partnership that constituted the child's family (such as step-parents) or anyone the child has been living with for at least three of the last five years can apply to the court for contact. With the permission of the court, grandparents and other relatives and the child himself can also apply.

FACTS

Contact Centres

Contact centres are intended to be child-friendly places that are not in either parent's home. They are often held in local community centres or church halls. A typical centre will be open twice each week and staffed by volunteers. Many will charge a fee for their services.

When parents attend contact centres it is usually because a court has decided that direct and unsupervised contact between the non-resident parent and the child might carry a risk of harm, either to the child or to the parent with care. Social workers, solicitors and CAFCASS officers can also make referrals independently. In some circumstances, parents can themselves arrange to use a contact centre, perhaps as a safe and neutral place where they can hand the children over for contact visits without themselves having to meet. However, there is an increasing shortage of contact centres in many areas, so there are often limits on who can use them and how often.

Visits that take place in a contact centre are called 'supervised contact' and there are some contact centres that specialise in providing professional, or at least skilled, supervision. What is usually provided, though, is more accurately described as 'supported contact', which means that there will be volunteers around who will generally oversee all visits taking place, making sure children are safe and adults behave appropriately, but nobody supervising individual contact arrangements.

'Contact between your child and their other parent':
https://www.gingerbread.org.uk/content/Advice

- A specific issue order is used when there is disagreement about particular aspects of children's upbringing, such as what school they go to or whether they should have a religious education.
- A prohibited steps order (PSO) is used to prevent the non-resident parent from making decisions about the child's upbringing which they would otherwise be entitled to make as part of normal parental responsibility. For example, a non-resident father may be prohibited from taking a child on holiday or

abroad, or taking him to spend time with another adult who is considered unsuitable.

- The existence of such an order also means that the resident parent can make important and urgent decisions on the child's behalf – such as those concerning medical treatment – without first seeking the agreement of the other parent.

Enforcing court orders

If you disagree with the terms of a court order you may be able to appeal against it. Appealing is difficult and complicated, and you will need legal advice, which will be expensive. However, appealing against an order is definitely preferable to ignoring or breaching it.

PART II: SEPARATING BETTER – OR WORSE

CHAPTER 5

KEEPING PARENTING AND PARTNERSHIP SEPARATE

There are almost as many ways of coping or failing to cope with parental separation and divorce as there are parents separating, and no book can sensibly suggest which will feel best, or least horrible, to you. However, it does seem that from the point of view of children – children in general, not specifically yours – there are better and worse ways of handling it, emotionally and practically. All the positive ways go together and so do all the negative ways. If (almost) everything you say and do for your children, and the arrangements you make for them, now and in the months or years ahead, fit with the 'better' group, you're making good choices. If a lot of it fits under worse, you're not.

The very best way to manage the break-up of a family so that it does the least possible long-term harm to children is to set your-selves to support the relationships each of you has with each of your children, and protect them from the failure of the relationship between the two of you. That's not an easy thing to do, and if you are a mother (or father) reading this when you are almost overwhelmed by hurt and fury at the children's father (or mother), it may seem downright impossible. Some people do manage it, though, and it is the most important effort you can make for your children right now, because it will affect every aspect of their lives both during and after your separation and divorce.

97

Whatever nasty adjectives may describe what your soon-to-be-ex is to you as a husband or partner, they do not describe what he is to the children as a father. For a start he's not 'ex' to them (you two may get divorced but he and the children remain father and children forever). And even if he is a bit rubbish as a dad, your children don't know it. He's just Daddy (or whatever word they've taken to). He's the only father they know and, bitter though it may be for you to acknowledge it right now, they love him as much (though differently) as they love you. You're going to be a lone parent, but that need not and should not mean that your children are going to be motherless or fatherless.

Feeling motherless or fatherless is terrible for a child of any age, but watching a parent struggling with the sadness, anger and depression of separation is also miserable for him or her. Many people believe that children don't notice or care what is happening to adults, that they are too self-centred and selfish to be concerned with anyone's feelings but their own. But the egocentricity of children is a misapprehension and an important one. When young children go on playing noisy games after you've told them you have a headache, it's not because they don't care about you, but because they haven't yet developed the empathy which lets them put themselves in your shoes and realise that lots of noise will make your headache worse. With any luck they don't even really know what 'headache' means. As children get older their demands for your attention, even when you are on the phone, are not because they are spoiled and care only about themselves, but because you are so much the centre of their lives that they find it hard to believe that they are not the entire centre of yours.

Children of all ages are extremely sensitive to parents' moods and feelings. The cues a baby uses are not the same as an older child's, of course, and the understanding a four-year-old brings to what is going on is not the same as an adolescent's, but whatever his age your child will sense it when either or both of you are unhappy and distracted or irritated and enraged with each other, and will worry about you both. Just as bereaved children mourn differently from adults and are sometimes thought to be heartless, children show this kind of worry in different ways from adults. Your sympathetic child may be more likely to bring you an extra-large beetle to stroke as to stroke your arm, but even if you're not keen on beetles it's important to recognise the gesture.

To make the best of what is inevitably a bad situation for the child, each of you needs to make a clear separation in your mind and in your behaviour between the adult-to-adult and the adult-to-child relationships in the family. If (and when) you can manage that, your child will know that the unhappiness she sees and senses is only adult business; the parenting business that is central to her life is still intact.

Yes, I know she loves her too. And Izzie loves her mum come to that. But she can't love her the way I do or she wouldn't have walked out would she? They say it's really rare for mothers to scarper and if one parent walks out it's usually the dad, but I'd never, never have done that. Never.

Father of girl, aged four

That brief quote makes it tragically clear that this father has not managed to separate his relationship with his wife from his child's relationship with her. At that point in the family upheaval he felt that he and his little daughter had been equally 'left' and that the loss of love for himself that led to the separation included the child. 'She can't love her the way I do' is not a good starting point for mutual parenting. In contrast, the next quote is.

We both love her to death. Always have. Always will, I guess. But we couldn't go on living and fighting together, and if one of us had to move out it was better for Emily that it was him.

Mother of girl, aged five

Even those few words suggest a fundamental difference between the relationships of the two couples. The father who is quoted first feels that he and his little daughter are both victims in the separation: both were 'left'. The mother who is quoted second, on the other hand, sees the marital break-up as separate business and being left in the home as the next step both parents thought best for the child.

Keeping your parenting apart from your disintegrating partnership is somewhat easier if you realise that children, whatever their ages, don't want to share or even hear about parents' man-to-woman relationships. They may love to hear stories about how you met, or the drive to hospital the night they were born, but they will resist and resent being made to recognise and think about your emotional and especially your sexual life with each other. That relationship is adult business, not children's. Using a child as a confidante is at best inappropriate, at worst sometimes close to abusive.

> *When we were at his house Dad did talk – would talk – about him and Mum and how much he missed her and how she'd betrayed him. It didn't make me sorry for him, it made me embarrassed, especially when it looked as if he was going to cry. One time he'd been drinking whisky and he got all emotional and started talking about getting lonely for her in bed. Yuck. That put me off both of them.*
>
> Girl, aged twelve

Do all you can to keep your hurt, sense of betrayal, loneliness and fury private from children, and keep the arguments and fights that belong to your failing adult relationship as quiet as you can.

It's almost as difficult and even more important to prevent what you feel now about your ex (let's say the children's father), as a partner, from changing what you've always felt about him as a father. If he was an OK dad before your adult relationship blew up, he still will be if circumstances (and you) allow him. If he's always been an active parent, loving and hands-on, you need to go on believing in his absolute reliability as a father, respecting his input into every aspect of the child's upbringing and enjoying their pleasure in each other. It isn't easy, but it is possible, especially if both of you feel at least some degree of joint responsibility for the breakdown of your relationship and if there isn't a third party closely involved. It's difficult enough to be positive about your child spending the weekend with the other parent, much more difficult if there's a substitute-you there too (see page 63).

When separating parents do manage to salvage intact not only their own but each other's parenting, they sometimes find that part of the lonely space left by the broken partnership has been filled with mutual parenting. That's the best possible gift they can make to their children.

His second affair threw up a lot of crap between us but even before it had settled I realised that he was still the only person in the world I could trust with the boys, the only person who'd drop everything for them in any kind of emergency and handle it, whatever it was, just the way I'd want. I had other people supporting me as a lone mum, but I'd think about dying, and what would happen to Luke and Larry if I did, and the thought of them going to live with their grandmother or one of their aunts gave me the absolute shudders. Their father is the only other person they 100 per cent love and who would bring them up the way we'd planned. So I didn't want him for me – let's face it, didn't want him in my bed any more – but I did want him for our children and that's dictated all our arrangements ever since.

Mother of two boys, aged four and eight

If Diane had been older maybe we'd have tried separate flats close by so she could pop in and out. But with her so little we

*weren't going to divide her up, so we divided ourselves up: split
the house. We have half each, she has it all. Lots of people,
like neighbours who aren't real friends, don't even know we're
divorced. Diane knows of course, but it really doesn't bother her.
Why should it? There's always a parent at home and there's
always supper in one of two kitchens and her own precious bed
waiting in her room.*

Father of girl, aged two during the divorce and now aged five

MUTUAL PARENTING

Mutual parenting is not at all the same as shared or equal parenting. Those terms usually refer to arrangements in which a child's time (and therefore care) is shared between mother and father and is dealt with in Chapter 7: 'Sharing Parenting'.

Mutual parenting means that whatever else is or is not going on in your relationship – today, this month or next year – you feel jointly committed to putting your children's wellbeing and happiness first and to protecting them as far as you can from the ill-effects of your separation. The most important word in that sentence is 'jointly'. Many separating mothers and many separating fathers say that they themselves put their children first, but not many of them credit each other with doing so or manage to do it together.

The most difficult aspect of making your children's wellbeing a mutual priority is that it involves you in being together, or at least in frequent communication, when you'd probably prefer to have nothing whatsoever to do with each other. What is more, if you are very bitter towards your ex you may find that although you are sure of your own commitment and good intentions towards the children, you struggle to believe in those of a person you are currently finding it impossible to tolerate or trust, let alone like. It is a worthwhile struggle, though, because conflict between the parents is known to be the very worst aspect of many children's experience of family breakdown: worse even than the actual separation.

Even leaving aside the stress of having to be in touch with an ex-partner, putting children first doesn't come easily to all separating parents – or to all parents in intact families, come to that. Seeing divorce as the way out of a marriage that's become miserable, some feel that they are entitled to make seeking their own happiness their priority:

> *It goes without saying that she matters and of course I'll see she's OK, but I don't see that she has to come first. This divorce is for me, to free me to be with someone I really love.*
>
> Mother of girl, aged two

Everyone is entitled to look for their own happiness, provided that happiness does not come at a disproportionately high cost to someone else. So while of course parents are entitled to seek their own happiness with or without new partners (greater happiness for at least one person is the point of separating, after all), they are surely not entitled to allow their separation and seeking to cost their children one iota more misery than it need. Parents (and indeed all adults) need to put children ahead of themselves, not only because it's nicer for children to be happy but also because children's happiness and wellbeing affects the way they are developing right now, the kind of people they will grow up to be and therefore the kind of society they will make when it's time for them to take over.

> *Yes, I do think separating is right for us but I also think that we are only entitled to do it if we can protect the kids from the fallout. In fact (does this sound horribly prissy?) I think we've sort of got to earn the end of our marriage by making sure of their parenting.*
>
> Mother of three girls, all under five

If you are having trouble deciding if you can manage mutual parenting, whether, for the children's sakes, you can each stand to be in cooperative touch rather than walking away from each other as well as from the marriage, don't rush. Give yourselves time to get over the shock of separation and then ask yourselves whether each of you would do as much to help the other with your joint children as you would do to help your sister or your best friend with hers.

- Would you phone him/expect him to phone you in the middle of the night if there was an emergency, such as one child needing to be taken to hospital and there being no one to care for the others?
- Would you discuss with him/expect him to discuss with you any worrying child behaviour, such as a three-year-old going back to nappies or a nine-year-old crying easily and often?
- Would you do your best/expect him to do his best to make the transfer from one parent to the other at the beginning and end of visits easy for the children?
- Would you cover for him/expect him to cover for you if one of you had forgotten a child's sports day or school play and didn't turn up? ('Mummy had to work late' rather than 'Mummy forgot'.)
- Would you pay attention to each other's opinions on important educational decisions such as keeping a child in nursery rather than school for an extra year, choosing a school, finding the money for a school trip or taking up a musical instrument?
- Would you pay attention to each other's views on managing children's behaviour (such as how best to handle tantrums or how much fuss to make about table manners), and try to agree on routines (such as bedtimes) and limits (such as not cycling without a helmet) so that the children had similar expectations and boundaries with each parent?

If the answer to all or most of those is 'yes' (or 'of course', 'no question' or 'what do you think?'), then you do have the foundations for mutual parenting.

A parent doesn't have to have been hands-on with the children to make parenting responsibilities a priority, although a father will become hands-on as soon as he finds himself in full charge, and his relationships with the children will change anyway as they get older. But while mutual parenting within an intact family can work on the basis of different gender roles – accepted by both parents and by the children – mutual parenting after a separation does require at least enough blurring of those roles that each parent can operate independently of the other. Giving equal headspace to the children is more important than being equally hands-on. A man whose fathering has been conventional/old-fashioned may have had very little practice at changing nappies, but as long as he realises that it matters to the toddler how nappies are changed, he can soon learn. The issue, as the points above suggest, is child-centredness.

The mother quoted below found it difficult to imagine her ex becoming child-centred, and it's easy to see why. But although they started from different points of view and with very different attitudes, these two almost managed successful mutual parenting:

Mark is a man's man. He likes women as playmates and kids
for status. I've never known him put the children ahead of his
own wishes, in fact finding time to spend with them among his
work and the tennis club was rare, and he always wanted me
to make babysitting arrangements so we could have adults-only
holidays or evenings out. He really doesn't like family treats
or celebrations. In fact I don't think he's really a family man,
so how can I take him seriously when he says all the divorce
business must put the kids first?

Mother of two girls, aged five and seven, and a boy, aged nine

The father, Mark, responded by saying that he felt that his main responsibility as a parent was to make generous and secure financial arrangements after the divorce. He planned to play a part in the children's lives by sharing decisions about their education and activities. He did also assume that once his ex was a lone parent it would be his responsibility to provide emergency back-up, although he reserved the right to do that 'by throwing my money at it rather than my time'. Although he had never seen much of the children he did realise that he was no longer even glimpsing them at the breakfast table, and he was looking for other ways of seeing them regularly within his own lifestyle. His most successful initiative was taking them for lessons at the tennis club each weekend, which they much enjoyed.

However, after more than a year it gradually became clear that mutual parenting wasn't working for Mark and his ex. The part that they couldn't manage was the part that is actually key: mother and father feeling genuinely supportive of each other in relation to the children and even retaining some respect for each other as parents. The children's mother had never respected Mark as a father and he had little respect for the role of mother. After two or three years they had to settle for the next best thing, which is not mutual but polite parenting.

POLITE PARENTING

Some couples understand the importance to children of their parents staying in close touch but find it impossible to manage – or even imagine – the two-way support that is the essence of mutual parenting. Fortunately, being unable wholeheartedly to support each other doesn't mean you have to be enemies. There are lesser degrees of contact and communication that demand much less friendship but still protect the children from the worst fall-out from the separation-bomb.

Establishing polite parenting usually depends on making relatively formal arrangements, not only about dividing up money and property and about which parent the child will live with after separation, but also about when and where and how the other parent will spend time with him. Since before a court will grant you a divorce or dissolve a civil partnership you have to show that you have made these arrangements (see page 84), you have to discuss them, and if you are both trying to be polite you may be able to work them out between you. Often, though, parents who are struggling with civility enlist the help of solicitors to make sure that these agreements leave nothing to chance (or to unwelcome discussion).

Some couples draw up amazingly detailed documents, including lists of rules to which each signs agreement, templates for telephone calls between them, and 'visit logs' that each parent must fill in before the child is transferred to the care of the other. But rigid plans backed by written documents can only be the bare bones of life after separation, and actually using them is likely to provide one parent with a weapon to use against the other ('It says you're to bring her back by six-thirty, not six-forty-seven'), so the hope must be that they won't be needed for long. Once you have been physically apart for a few months, during which neither of you has broken the agreements nor done anything to offend, the flexibility you need and the communication it takes can usually creep in. It's not unheard of for a polite parenting set-up eventually to become something close to mutual.

Sometimes, though, parents have issues with each other that make even polite parenting impossible. Perhaps, for example, a father is determined to have easy access to a small child and 'fair shares of her time', despite the fact that while the marriage lasted, his fathering was of the 'bedtime story when he got home early enough' kind and the child has never been separated from her mum.

Come on Maria, you've always played up what hard work it is looking after Melanie, but how hard can it be?

Father of girl, aged two

If he has never before taken sole responsibility for the child – meals and play, bath times, bedtimes and bad dreams, squabbles and safety measures – the mother may find it impossible to agree to regular overnight visits until he has got to know the child, while he is determined not to 'settle for anything less'. Any attempts at cooperation are stillborn.

Some fathers and mothers have always had different views on aspects of their children's upbringing. While they lived together one parent balanced the other and their differences didn't seem insurmountable, but once they are apart neither parent can feel fully supportive and trusting of the other so that they can share polite parenting:

There are things to do with the kids that we just don't agree on. Like she's really against ordinary medicine and into all that alternative stuff. We've often argued about it and a few times I've actually taken one of them to the GP against her wishes 'cause I thought the child needed antibiotics. What will happen when I'm not around?
Father of two boys, aged three and four, and one girl, aged eight

He's a good father but he's nobody's darling daddy. Bit uptight. Bit cold. Very religious. He never interfered with the way I carried on with her, but she'll not get much fun or much loving if I'm not there.

Mother of girl, aged four

Being polite is even more difficult for a parent who feels that the other is (or might be) a negative influence in a child's life. For example, if one parent has always found it difficult to meet or even tolerate a child's special needs, the other parent may not even want to contemplate situations where parent and child are alone together.

> *When Charles was a baby his father could cope. But changing nappies on 'a big boy' and helping him feed himself with a spoon is beyond him. He says it turns him up and I've always done it. If the two of them were alone together I don't think he'd leave Charles dirty or hungry, but I do think he'd make it obvious he was disgusted and I wouldn't trust him not to try and force Charles to do things that are beyond him.*
>
> Mother of boy, aged six

These are not the kinds of issue that both parents are likely to reach agreement on without help, but that doesn't mean they have to cause a fight. If a basic plan is arrived at, with help, perhaps, from a mediator or a solicitor, such that the children will live with the father in the first example, the mother in the other two, and in each instance have daytime (rather than overnight) contact at weekends with the other parent, there is no reason why putting the plan into action should not be done politely.

CHAPTER 6

TRYING TO GET CHILDREN TO TAKE SIDES

'ALIENATION': WHAT IT MEANS AND WHY IT MATTERS

The very worst thing you can do to your children during the horrible months around your separation is to try to put them off the other parent. You'll hear this called 'alienation' by solicitors or social workers and in court. Now that we know how important it is for children to be as closely involved as possible with both parents, alienation is recognised as dreadfully damaging. In some parts of the world, including the United States, it is actually against the law for one parent to set out to spoil a child's relationship with or feelings about the other.

Deliberate alienation uses children as weapons in an adult battle, making them even more its victims. From children's point of view this is the most damaging, the worst way their mothers and fathers can react to separation, and it leads to the very opposite of the best: to 'broken parenting' instead of to 'mutual' or even 'polite parenting'.

ALIENATION BY CIRCUMSTANCE OR DEFAULT

If you're a mother or father whose partner has left the family home, it's all too easy to put your child off him or her even without meaning to. You are upset, miserable, furious – whatever your exact emotions, they are probably pretty strong – and however hard you try to conceal your feelings your child will sense them. Because you are there and the child is upset because the other parent is not there, he may well take your side, turning against your soon-to-be ex. That scenario is especially likely if, far from being part of a long process of marriage breakdown with one parent's eventual departure mutually anticipated if not exactly agreed, the separation was a shock to you and you still hope, or at least wish, that the marriage may be glued together again. Children almost invariably want that too, so that puts the two of you on the same side (and in the same house), with the other parent on the other side and somewhere else.

Mum kept crying. She cried a lot. I hated her crying. And Dad wasn't ever there to huggle her better. And when I said to her, 'Let's go and get him' she said, 'He just doesn't want to be here any more', and I'm here so that meant he didn't want to be with me either.

Boy, aged six; his answer to the question: 'What made you so angry with your dad?'

If the break-up was over an affair, your child will soon gather that and may not easily forgive what he or she will probably see as a straightforward theft of one parent from the other. Children who need to blame someone find it far easier to blame an individual who isn't either parent but a cuckoo in the family nest. If the relationship that tips your marriage into separation should prove long-lasting, establishing a good relationship between the parent's new lover and the children may be bedevilled by their continued resentment. Meantime, the parent who has been left alone will almost always attract more of a child's (and everyone else's) sympathy, so unless you really work to prevent it the whole situation will push the children and their other parent apart.

It's miserably easy for a baby or toddler to become alienated from an absent parent – let's say it's her father who has left, because the statistics say that's more likely than her mother – just because he isn't there. Unless the two of you make a point of father and child seeing each other regularly and often from the very beginning of the separation, their relationship will loosen instead of getting increasingly close, and eventually it will lapse. If you actually want that to happen – perhaps because you want to punish the father or perhaps because you just want nothing whatsoever to do with him – all you have to do is keep them mostly apart for several months. A shockingly large number of women do just that, perhaps not realising that their beloved child suffers at least as much as her dad.

If a baby, under a year old, doesn't spend any time with her father for weeks or months, the attachment between them that should have been building up towards a peak in the second year doesn't grow. She will not 'forget' him. Whatever relationship she had with her father while he lived in the same home played a part in the way her brain and nervous system developed in her first months, so he is forever part of who she is. But the area of her brain that stores memories is not yet developed enough for her consciously to remember him for long. If he is out of sight for months he will also be out of conscious mind. She will not be aware of missing him because the space in her life that he used to occupy will close up.

It's different if a child is two or three years old or more when the break-up happens. If he has made a close bond with the father during his short life before the separation, he will be very aware of father's departure and absence and at the beginning will probably badly miss specific things they used to do together. But over a few months he will get used to his father not being there and adapt to the new lifestyle. If a reconciliation brought Daddy home, he would probably still be delighted, but after months apart suddenly being expected to leave Mum and home and go out with him (perhaps because the father has at last gained legal access) is a different matter. Daddy doesn't mean anything clear-cut to him. In fact, he may not really understand who this man is. He may be shy and reluctant. A toddler's very natural hanging back – probably with both arms firmly around his mother's thigh – is a potent weapon in an undeclared alienation war. His father, who was looking forward to excited greetings and hugs from his child, will feel devastatingly sad and rejected, especially if he has been fighting hard for the right to spend time with him. His mother will probably feel vindicated, or at least excused for her part in keeping them apart. Clearly the child does not want to be with the father, and surely he should not be forced? By the time that question gets back to conciliation or court, another few weeks, even months, will have passed, and that child, now three years old, has little remaining conscious memory of his dad.

Yet another year or two on, at four or five, that shyness and reluctance to go with a scarcely known visiting father may take on a desperate intensity, with the child tearful and panicky when the father comes to pick him up. The extreme reaction is usually not to being with the father but to being taken away from the mother. Look at it from the child's point of view: Daddy left, so how can he be sure that if he takes his eyes off Mummy she won't leave too (see page 165)?

Mary's not four yet. She can't get her arms right around the pillar-box that stands outside her front gate, but it's a sturdy, familiar landmark and she's going to hang on to it whatever all the grown-ups say about Daddy taking her for a treat. I think

she knows she's being conned. Treats have Mummy in them. Or
me. Or maybe Lucy's mum (she's good at treats).

Grandmother of girl, aged three

A scene like that is agony for everybody. For the child, who is sub-merged in the worst kind of fear there is for a child that age: fear of losing her mother. For the mother, who hates to see her so upset (and hates the father for making her that way). And, of course, for the father, who is being made to feel like an insensitive brute for wanting to spend time with the daughter he loves. Probably nobody meant father and child to become alienated, but they have.

If a child's relationship with his or her father is protected and facilitated from the beginning, even though the two of them don't live in the same house any more, painful separation scenes like this can usually be avoided. But not always. Separation anxiety is ordinary in one- to three-year-olds and by no means unusual for another two or three years, especially when family stresses make children feel insecure. But although it is not unusual for 'contact arrangements' to blow up, it is vital not to abandon them altogether. For babies, tod-dlers and pre-school children there is one particular solution that's guaranteed from the child's point of view, though it can be tough on parents: let her father come to the child's home to spend time with her and, if necessary, have Mum hanging around in the background so she feels safe.

I couldn't have him in the house, playing with Mary as if he
was still family; seeing my things; drinking my tea as if he lived
there . . .

Mary's mother

Understandable though these feelings are, they belong to the moth-er's relationship as woman to man, not to Mary's relationship with her father.

If you really cannot bring yourself to let your ex spend time in the home, even though you can see that it's the best way for your small child to spend happy time with him, a compromise may work. If there is a grandparent, aunt or friend the child feels close to, and whose house she often visits, meeting her father there may enable her to enjoy being with him. Meeting at Grandmother's house worked for Mary, and when she went away on holiday Mary and her father were made welcome by Lucy's mum.

'Enjoy' is the key point, of course. If going out with Dad floods a child with anxiety and she is more or less forced to go, she will get minimal pleasure from this visit and, remembering her own anxious feelings, may dread the next. On the other hand, the more she enjoys whatever time she spends with her father and looks forward to seeing him again, the more self-sustaining their relationship will be.

Using your child as a go-between

If you are not seeing your ex but your child is, it's very convenient to use him as a messenger and very tempting to extract information from him. Don't. Even if you and your ex are on 'polite' terms, and the messages you send are entirely practical and the questions you ask are completely casual (How was Daddy today? Was he cheerful?), being used as a go-between mixes the child into the failed marital relationship when he ought to be allowed to think only about the successful parental one. If he wants to tell you what he's been doing, that's great (How was your day?), but don't ask him about his father; he'll volunteer anything he wants you to know.

If you really need to communicate with your ex, just do it. A generation ago that was far more difficult than it is now. Thanks to mobiles, phoning doesn't mean a landline, specific times of day and the risk of his lover picking up. If you don't want to phone because you don't want to speak to him, you can send a text or an email. If there are things you need to show him – documents, items in catalogues you're hoping the children can have for Christmas – using Skype or social media can save you the time and emotional effort of meeting face to face, and save you money too. However you choose to do it, your children's day-to-day wellbeing depends on their two parents being willing and able to communicate and to keep grown-up stuff between the two of them.

> *My mum really tried not to pry, not even to ask questions when I'd been out with Dad. But the atmosphere kind of stank of unasked questions and it got worse as I got older. One day – it must have been about a year ago, so I'd have been thirteen – I'd been out with him and when I got home Mum asked if I'd had a nice time, and that was OK: I said yes it had been fine. But then she asked me how my dad was and I managed to say he was fine, too. But then she tried one more question (the one she'd been building up to all along, as if I didn't realise that): how did his new job seem to be going? And I just blew up and told her 'If you really want to know, ask him yourself.'*
>
> Boy, aged fourteen

The less friendly, or even polite, the terms you are on, the worse it is for your child to play go-between, because every message will convey subtle criticism. The child will pick up on that and feel that he's being forced to share it.

'Tell your dad not to forget it's your concert next Saturday' sounds harmless, but it isn't: it clearly suggests to the child that his father is likely to forget an event that's important to him. Almost all 'reminders' also subtly convey the superiority over the recipient of the parent who sends them. I know when sports day or half-term is because I'm the parent in the know; he won't know unless I tell him and won't remember unless I remind him.

Even people who are not friends can email, so the 'if you have something to say to each other, do it directly' rule still holds. But do remember that when it comes to keeping track of nursery or school dates and events, each of you has an equal right to be kept informed by the school. If the school still communicates via those pieces of paper that end up crumpled in the bottom of your child's bag, a copy should routinely go in the post to the other parent. If that isn't happening, it's because nobody has told the school that the child's two parents live apart. Do it. If the school uses email, or expects parents to view its website, make sure the office has both addresses.

ANGRY ALIENATION AND ITS USE AS A WEAPON IN ADULT CONFLICT

A parent who lets a child get involved in the adult war that's raging in and around the household, or even deliberately uses her as a weapon against her ex, probably doesn't mean their child any harm. She may be one of many women who feel that, unlike being a mother, being a father is an earned privilege that men can lose through bad behaviour, and who don't think about the spin-off effects on the children. Or she may be so full of fury at the man who has betrayed her that she thinks she's actually right to protect the child from her father.

However well-meaning her motives, and whatever the individual circumstances, deliberate alienation is wrong, and the lengths to which some alienating parents will go and the damage they cause to their children are truly shocking.

When a father has left the family home, some mothers will lie and cheat to keep him and their child from speaking to or seeing each other, and to lessen the father in the child's eyes:

To father: He can't come to the phone; he's in the bath.
To child: No, it was not your father. Do you really think he's going to bother phoning?

> *To father: She told me to tell you she doesn't want to speak to you.*
> *To child: Yes, it was him. Drunk as per usual. I told him he wasn't fit to speak to you.*
> *To father on doorstep: They're not coming out with you; they've gone to their nan's.*
> *To children: You didn't want to go with him and leave me all by myself did you?*

Examples such as these may sound trivial, but cumulatively they are toxic.

Some parents, men as well as women, will share their own hateful feelings with children, encouraging them not only to see the absent one in a bad light, but also to lose faith in the family relationships they used to take for granted:

> *She's never been any good; I never would have married her 'cept you was on the way. She's nothing of a mum. Yes, of course you thought you loved her, but that's where she's clever. She turns on the charm and people believe it.*

Perhaps cruellest of all, some parents play a bid for sympathy from children who love them, making it seem disloyal of them to love the other parent:

> *Don't you leave me too . . . You're all I've got. Every time I see you hug him it's like someone stabbed me . . . We're all right together aren't we? We don't need him.*

Non-resident parents are in a weak position compared with the parents children live with. A lot of them are sufficiently intimidated by this kind of behaviour that the alienation actually works and they gradually stop visiting.

At the time I just couldn't stand it. Going down every Saturday
– three trains and £30-odd quid – and then finding that the
kids weren't there – or she said they weren't – or they were there
but she made such a performance about where I was taking
them that she really made it sound like I was going to kidnap
them. Once they were crying and saying they didn't want to
come with me, she'd get all reasonable and say, 'It's only Daddy.
I'm sure he'll take you on a nice walk', but it was too late then.
The last time she actually said, 'I'm so sorry Marty' (all posh-
like), 'I'm doing my best but it's not my fault they don't love you
any more.' She's lucky I didn't slap her.

I wish now I'd gone on somehow. Maybe I should have gone
back to the solicitor. But that cost a bomb and anyway I was –
how to put it? – offended. These are my kids and she shamed
me with them and now it's almost two years since I saw them
and it's too late.

Father of girl, now aged eight, and boy, now aged six

When a non-resident parent will not be put off but is insistent
on seeing the children, and especially if both parents have been
through mediation or the non-resident parent does go and seek
advice from a solicitor, the resident parent may become aware that
the law will not allow her to go on refusing to let the children see
their father without a very good reason. At this point she may go to
CAFCASS or to a solicitor saying that there is reason for thinking
the child might be at risk with his father; that the non-resident parent's environment would be unsafe or a bad influence (alcoholism,
drug addiction and mental illness may be mentioned) or that, given
the opportunity, the other parent will take the child away, possibly
out of the country.

Such claims may or may not be accurate, but because they
are about child protection (the court's principal concern) they
will have to be investigated and legal aid will be provided. Even

if the children are not old enough to understand what the mother is saying about father, putting forward such accusations almost always has an alienating effect. This is true even if they are without foundation and the father totally denies them all, seeing them as part of a deliberate attempt to alienate the children from him. Once he has been accused, he cannot simply continue to insist on seeing the children – and certainly must not attempt to do so without the mother's knowledge or against her wishes. Instead he will have to apply to the court for a contact order. The date for hearing such an order may be set months ahead, which, unless the father is success-ful in getting an immediate interim contact order with the help of CAFCASS or a solicitor, could mean that the child does not see him at all during that period and as a result their relationship is further damaged.

Sometimes the claims a resident parent makes against the other parent strike him as entirely outrageous. If they are produced out of the blue, having never been mentioned during preceding months of legal wrangling, it may be difficult for him to understand why anyone takes any notice. However, if there is the least chance that the father has been abusive, he cannot be allowed contact with the child until the matter has been investigated. On the other hand, the court recognises the importance to children of contact with both parents, and must try to balance the two. Supervised contact, at a contact centre (see p. 91) or at the home of an approved relative, is the court's best available compromise. However insulting it may feel to the parent, and however inadequate to the children's needs, it is better than no contact at all and it is usually assumed to be temporary. If all goes well, the non-resident parent can apply after a few months to have contact liberalised.

Whatever the truth of the accusation or the eventual outcome of proceedings, allegations of sexual abuse ruin lives. Not only the lives of men whose ex-partners have accused them of abus-ing their mutual children, but also the lives of the children whose relationships with their fathers will never recover. An allegation of sexual abuse can be dismissed as groundless, found unproven, even withdrawn, but it cannot be unmade. Men, even some whose ex-wives never really believed their own accusations but made them so as to keep access to a minimum, have lost jobs and friends as well as their children.

It wasn't really my fault. I didn't say he had, I only said he might. Anyway I didn't actually mean it. I just didn't want him taking my girls away from me every weekend. Somehow it got around, though, and the children were interviewed and the school knew and then I absolutely tried to stop it but I couldn't. In the end Eric was pushed out of his job – he was manager of a local supermarket – and his new woman walked out on him and he can't pay what he's meant to in maintenance.

Mother of two girls, aged six and nine

AVOIDING ALIENATION WHEN AGREEMENT SEEMS IMPOSSIBLE

If you are really convinced that it is important to your children to have the best possible relationship with both parents and you are therefore really determined to avoid alienating them from your ex – let's say the mother – you can do it, even if there is no room for agreement or even politeness between you. There are arrangements that will ensure that your child can have contact with her without risk, and there are people and organisations who can help you to make them.

When one parent thinks the other is unfit

If you genuinely believe that your ex-partner is unfit to take sole charge of the children you will obviously try to make sure that doesn't happen. Allegations of abuse, addiction or dangerous neglect may seem the easiest way, but quite apart from their immorality, inaccurate or wildly exaggerated accusations may damage rather than protect the children. If you avoid alienating the children from her, a parent may still be able to have a loving relationship with them even though she cannot take care of them on her own, and while of course their safety and wellbeing is your first priority, ensuring they have the best possible relationship with the other parent comes close behind.

How easy or difficult it is to make arrangements that meet both those demands mostly depends on your own relationship with the other parent. If she recognises her own shortcomings as a parent in sole charge, is as anxious as you are about the children's safety and is grateful to you for encouraging contact with them, you may be able to make arrangements between you. That may sound like a very big 'if', but it does sometimes happen:

At the moment she's in rehab. She's an addict to just about any mind-altering stuff you can think of. She seems to get hooked on whatever's available and some of the mixtures she's taken in the last couple of years have been really dangerous. Last time I was away for work there was a fire. She didn't even wake but the kids got her out. Six and four they were then. That was it for pretending she was in charge of them. Luckily she knows. She loves them and she knows she can't be sure to keep them safe, so she hasn't fought me. The kids see her at weekend visiting and when she comes out she'll probably come and see them here or, come the summer, they could go to the park with friends. She can't mother them but she's still their mother.

Father of boy, aged seven, and girl, aged five

I divorced him when they were only three and one year old, so I guess I could have sort of dropped him out of their lives. He was an alcoholic and family life just wasn't possible, but he

*was – and is – a nice man and he loved them and still does, so
I didn't want to take all that away. He sees them every week
and always has. I wouldn't let them go away and stay with him
because he mightn't be responsible, but he knows that himself
and wouldn't ask. But they're perfectly safe going out with him
in the daytime. They're movie-buffs, all of them.*

Mother of two girls, aged six and eight

Of course most parents are not so accepting of being judged 'unfit' and many are extremely reluctant to accept restrictions that their ex-partners try to impose on their contact with the children, especially if there is no objective evidence against them, such as a relevant medical condition, criminal record, police warning or referral to social services. The most frequent focus for anxiety is overnight visits (see page 145) and it is these that many parents – like the two quoted above – seek to prevent. Sometimes the resident parent's long and intimate knowledge of the other parent is enough to worry him or her. For instance, if a father has been irritable and not at all child-centred during the marriage, the mother may know that he will have no idea how to cope with the child's evening and bedtime routine and that he might lose his temper with the child if things go wrong.

If you are generally managing polite if not mutual parenting, you may be able to talk through and resolve anxieties and arrive at mutually acceptable living arrangements for the children and visiting plans for the non-resident parent. However, that parent, let's say it's the father, may find himself caught up in a vicious circle in which his anger and humiliation at not being trusted with his own child builds up to such a point that he breaks the agreed arrangements and so confirms his ex's suspicions about his untrustworthiness. The breaches may be trivial – bringing the child back a few minutes late, perhaps, or buying him a forbidden snack – but sometimes they are more serious:

We agreed that he could take her to spend Saturday with his mother. The second time he did it he rang me to say they'd missed the train and would have to stay over. It was just an excuse. He did it on purpose. I just can't trust him to stick to what we've worked out.

Mother of girl aged four

If it proves impossible for both of you to honour shared arrangements, you may need the help of the court in imposing them.

When one parent has been shown to be unfit

If your ex was physically abusive to one of the children, or to you – perhaps in sight of the children – or has been shown to have sexually abused one of the children, or if he has been convicted of some other appalling crime, it's entirely understandable if you want him to have nothing further to do with you or the children. But while wanting to airbrush him right out of all your lives and what is left of your family is understandable from your point of view, it is not desirable from your children's. Hopefully, when your fury and disgust at his behaviour begins to let up, you will see that you can't and shouldn't get rid of him altogether, and that the law won't let you.

First the 'can't'. Whatever this man has done, he exists. However much you wish it weren't so, he is your children's biological father. To wipe him out of their lives, you'd have to be prepared to tell whopping lies to the children when eventually they ask about their dad, and to friends and neighbours too. If he left and you remarried when the children were tiny, you might pretend your second husband, their stepfather, is their father. If the children were old enough when he left to remember him, you might tell them he is dead. But quite apart from the rights and wrongs of this sort of deception, you would certainly get caught out eventually and that would be the end of trust in your family.

Now the 'shouldn't'. All children have a deep-seated need to know about their parents and where they came from. You only have to look on the internet to see the huge numbers of people who spend hours trying to trace their lost beginnings. Most people accept that need in adopted or looked-after children, and nowadays we take the trouble to be open with them so that they can ask questions when they're ready and deal with truthful answers even if they're painful. That need is exactly the same for children like yours whose fathers are absent because they are abusive or have been convicted of other crimes.

Mothers shouldn't try to airbrush even abusive fathers out of children's lives, but that does not mean that they should invite those fathers in. If you are genuinely afraid of your ex, you have every right to refuse to see him and the family court system will support you. But if he goes to the court asking to be allowed contact with the children, the court will not automatically refuse it, whatever he did in the past, because being a father is not conditional on good behaviour and children have a right to the best possible relationship with both parents.

The court will call experts to explore the father's motives for seeking contact (does he really love them or is he trying to use them to keep power over you?). Those experts will seek to understand what happened in your ex's childhood, and to assess the dynamics of the family. A good court assessment can go a long way to explaining what might have gone wrong in the parental relationship and to helping work out if their father should see the children or have any contact with them. Those assessments will also help to find out how the children really feel about their dad. Research shows that children are often so desperate not to hurt the parent they live with that they will say what they know she wants to hear rather than what they actually feel. That can mean that yours say bad things about their father, and say they don't want any contact with him, when, truthfully, like it or not, they love him.

After an expert assessment the court will decide whether your ex should be allowed to have contact with the children and, if so, what kind and how much.

CHAPTER 7

SHARING PARENTING

TOWARDS CHILD-CENTREDNESS

When partners separate they stop being a couple but they don't stop being parents. No matter who left whom or why, neither the father nor the mother is any less a parent than before the break-up. It took two of you to make your babies and neither of you could ever stop being their parent even if you wanted to. Being closely in contact with both their parents during and after family breakdown is enormously important to children. And that's increasingly widely recognised in family law. Indeed, legal recognition of parents' equality is mandatory in the USA, Australia and the UK. But if it is now generally accepted that mothers and fathers are equally parents, it is not generally agreed what being a parent means in that context: what role follows the fact. If you are equally parents, does that automatically mean that your parenting is equal, and if so, is that equality a matter of quality, quantity or both? In Australia, mandatory legal recognition of the equality of separating parents was widely interpreted to mean both: fathers were to be viewed and dealt with in the courts as equally import- ant as mothers and to have equal rights of access to the children. In the US – and now in the UK – the emphasis is on quality and on children's rather than parents' rights. Fathers' equal impor- tance is mostly a matter of being as concerned and responsible for the children's wellbeing as the mother and, in the long run, equally important to them. It does not necessarily mean spending equal time in hands-on care.

Before the court will grant you a divorce – even an undefended one – you must say which of you the child or children will live with (the 'resident parent'); how much and where they will see the other parent (the 'non-resident or contact parent'), and which of you will pay for what. But formal answers to those questions from the court are largely legal formalities. Provided that separating parents are in agreement with each other and submit a joint, uncontested plan, they can make whatever actual arrangements they please.

Nobody else cares whether the children really are spending more time with the 'resident parent' than the other, and of course there is nothing to stop parents from sharing monetary benefits or arranging maintenance between them. So the two of you have the freedom and responsibility to answer those crucial questions:

- Where and with whom are the children going to live?
- Where is maintenance money going to come from?
- And when and how is the non-resident parent to see them?

Those questions are easier to ask than to answer. Making arrangements for what you will hear solicitors or social workers call 'contact' or 'access' for the parent whom children don't actually live with, and making sure that both of you stick to them, is one of the most important and most difficult parts of post-separation life.

MAKING PARENTING PLANS

King Solomon's twenty-first-century solutions
Everyone surely has to accept that mothers and fathers are equally parents; it is a biological fact after all. But equal, or shared, parenting is a different matter and widely misunderstood to mean that a

mother and father ought to have as near half-shares of their children as is practically possible. Sometimes that means half of the children: cutting a family of siblings in two, with one child going with Mum and another with Dad. More often it means cutting each child's time and lifestyle down the middle so that she spends roughly half her time with one parent and half with the other. None of that is quite as horrible as King Solomon's suggestion that the baby over whom two women were quarrelling should be cut in two so that they could have half each, but as the wise king guessed, the possibility of the baby being killed revealed the real mother, who renounced her claim, in order to save him.

Modern versions of sharing out children are fortunately not life-threatening, but unfortunately often appear less threatening to a child's wellbeing than they actually are, so that once they are in place parents don't feel the need to think again. Think carefully before you embark on trying to make a fair division of your children, or of one child's time and presence, between the two of you. Your children are not sharable commodities like the family dog or the money in the savings account. That's never the best approach to sharing parenting, and is often seriously damaging to children whose lives end up salami-sliced.

All over the Western world there are children who are uprooted at regular and frequent intervals from one parent's home to the other's, and they may never be sure which is home for them. There are 'access arrangements' that change children over mid-week so that they spend Sunday night to Wednesday afternoon in one household, Wednesday night to Sunday afternoon in the other. Some children spend alternate whole weeks with each parent and some alternate school terms. Probably the most common arrangement is for children to spend weekdays with one parent, and weekends (sometimes alternate weekends) with the other. This last arrangement is popular with adults because if the weekend is counted as Friday afternoon to Monday morning, it gives parents almost 'fair shares' of the children, and that division often fits with patterns of children's school and the non-resident parent's working hours. Such an arrangement may or may not be popular with children. In some (usually well-to-do) communities, it's not unusual to live, and work, in one place (usually thought of as home) and retreat to a holiday place for weekends. If it makes a life-pattern that a child settles into and eventually enjoys, this plan may work well for everyone, but don't take it for granted. As with every other aspect of coping better with family breakdown, you need to think about your own individual children:

All my school sports things are on Saturday, and now I'm in year 6 I'm in the teams. Football now; cricket in the summer. When they said about going to my dad at weekends I did try to say about it, but they didn't really take much notice. Dad said he'd drive me to school on Saturdays, but we only did it once 'cause he said it was too far. I asked Mum if I could just go to Dad's on Saturday afternoon after the matches are over, but she said that wouldn't be fair, as Dad would only have me for one night. I think this way is not very fair on me.

Boy, aged ten

Mum gets all the homework hassles and washing uniform and driving to after-school stuff. We don't ever get to see each other in the daytime 'cause I'm at school, and we don't get to go out or have much fun time together in the evenings because it's always school again the next day. Sometimes I wish I could be with my dad when it's maths homework and be with my mum for a Saturday's shopping.

Girl, aged twelve

Even when routine week-by-week arrangements are comfortable for children as well as adults, King Solomon often reappears on high days and holidays. Many children must eat two Christmas dinners – often one on the day and the other on Boxing Day – and can only have school friends to their birthday parties every other year because on the alternate years it's the other parent's turn and the birthday celebration is too far away for school friends to come. Dividing up these special days is very difficult (maybe heartbreaking would be a better word) and very individual, but it matters to children, There are some suggestions from parents in Chapter 9.

1f King Solomon-like approaches to sharing parenting such as these are working for you and you are pretty well overwhelmed with the adult aspects of your separation, you may not even take the time to wonder if this is the best possible arrangement for your child or children. The non-resident parent – nine out of ten times, the father – often wants his 'fair share' of the children at almost any cost. He may feel – and advisers, from his mother to his solicitor, may tell him – that it's his right. Some fathers in this position even worry that settling for less than the nearest possible to a fifty-fifty division of children's time and presence might make his ex or the children themselves feel that he didn't care about them. As the resident – and now single – parent, you might prefer the children to live with you full time but be able to see the 'justice' of their father's case. Equally, though, you may be keen for the children to spend time with their father so that he shares the childcare burden and gives you predictable stretches of child-free time and the opportunity to get a new life going.

It works for me because I know exactly when he'll be with me and when I can have time off from mothering without having to pay a babysitter.

Mother on half-week care arrangement

It's OK. He's in my diary for the rest of term. We don't have to meet or discuss it. It's not perfect though – a bit rigid already

131

and that'll get worse when he's older. Already it's tricky keeping to it in the holidays when he wants to have particular kids over and he is in the wrong place. It would work better if we lived even closer together. High days are tricky too. Does he just spend his birthday with whichever parent he happens to be with on the day it falls? And Christmas – well we've already had one of those and it was miserable.

Her ex

I'd just like to live somewhere and visit the other place. Other kids go home; I go to my dad's or to my mum's.

Their son, aged eight

It's understandable that scenarios like these can be tempting, but they can never be acceptable, because they do not allow for children's feelings and choices. Children need to live through family breakdown as themselves, rather than as their parents' treats or burdens.

The life of each of your children belongs to him or her, not to either or both of you. It is the break-up of your marriage or other adult partnership that has made it necessary to formalise parenting into something shared between the two of you as individuals rather than enjoyed by you both as a couple, and in this situation it is your child's rights that are in question rather than yours. It is every child's right to maintain the best possible relationship with each parent and it is your joint responsibility to facilitate that as best you can.

Parents, children and parenting plans are individual, so no outsider – or even paid adviser – can tell you exactly what you should arrange. However, in the light of recent research, there are some basic recommendations and pitfalls that really do seem to apply to parents and children in general: parents in civil partnerships or same-sex marriages as well as heterosexual married couples, and adopted as well as biological children from infants to students.

Most of them have been discussed in earlier chapters, but the ones that are most important to your immediate practical planning and decision making are summarised here.

- Children's current and future happiness and wellbeing should be central to whatever parenting plans you make. Understandably a parent sometimes demands to know why: 'Why should children have priority? What about my happiness? Doesn't that matter just as much?' Of course both parents' happiness matters – indeed it is probably a search for some kind of happiness for at least one of you that led to the break-up of your family – but where your happiness and your children's happiness are at odds, children's must come first because while you are already formed adults, their lifelong development and their adult personalities, achievements and relationships are all ahead of them and depend on their emotional wellbeing through childhood. Having their family disintegrate and their parents living apart will in itself make children anxious and unhappy, of course, which is why it's not something any loving parent undertakes lightly. But by understanding which aspects of the new situation are most upsetting for this particular child at this particular time, and working to avoid or modify those even if you have to do so at your own expense, you can do a great deal to soften the impact.
- For many children the most important aspect of their parents' separation is not the obvious one – a parent moving out of the home to live elsewhere – but their mother and father's ongoing relationship, or lack of it. In fact, most children are more upset by the hateful atmosphere and endless arguments (or worse) that surround family breakdown than they are by the separation itself. The least traumatic parental separation for children is one in which the mother and father can remain respectful of each other as joint parents even though they reject each other as partners. The most destructive separation is one where the couple's

relationship becomes so toxic that one or both parents try to put the children off the other one and to persuade them to take sides (see page 116).

However mutual the parenting you are struggling towards, there will certainly be upsets, especially at the beginning of the separation. When you are trying to get your toddler to bed and he's alternately hitting out and clinging to you, it's desperately depressing to realise that he's missing Daddy's bedtime routine and stories and that yours aren't a satisfactory substitute. And when it's Friday night and you've made the especially nice supper that family tradition demands, but the older children turn sulky and unhelpful, it's demoralising to realise that a special Friday night supper was a family tradition and that although you've provided the meal, they're still missing the tradition. There will probably be many times like these when, however hard you are both trying to be supportive of each other as parents, it's impossible not to be angry and/or guilty on your children's behalf because you can see that they are suffering from the breakdown of their family and you know that the two of you brought it upon them. In the long term, though, rage and remorse for what's past won't help as much as thinking positively about the future. When the current storms die down, your separation need not prevent your children from being happy. Many children in so-called 'intact' families grow up and flourish while one parent works away from home for substantial periods of time or while securely married parents choose to occupy separate homes and visit each other. If there is a single, overwhelming difference between those children and yours it is that their parents are united though apart, and their children know it. You two are not united (and your children know it), but mutual parenting can come to mean that you are at one where they are concerned: that you parent together although you're apart.

Assessing and understanding each child's happiness and

wellbeing is crucial. It depends, of course, on their ages and stages of development and on careful observation of their behaviour. A teenager can and should be consulted about plans that involve him, and he may often be allowed to choose. A baby cannot choose, and her contentment with arrangements can only be judged by paying careful attention to her behaviour and not being too ready to ascribe everything undesirable to teething. Between those extremes, a three-year-old's distress at the prospect of going to spend a weekend away from her mum, or a six-year-old's sudden anxiety about going to school, should certainly be heard and carefully thought about, but should not always be directly acted upon, as immediate happiness and long-term wellbeing may not be the same. Often, though, immediate happiness and long-term wellbeing are the same, and if your eight- or eleven-year-old feels able to talk to you and sure that you will hear, he may tell you what he is missing most; she may tell you what keeps making her cry, and you may be able to put sticking plaster on the worst wounds.

Parenting plans need to be regular and predictable enough that all concerned – adults as well as children – can rely on them and come to take them for granted instead of wasting time and energy planning (and arguing) week by week. If it is part of the agreement that you will drive the children to meet up with their father each Sunday (perhaps because the family car has stayed with you), doing so must be a real commitment; and if father is due to visit at a particular time on a particular day, he must be there more or less on the dot, always.

But within the regularity that will help children come to feel safe and secure in the new arrangements, there also needs to be some flexibility, both week by week and in the long term, and this is yet another instance of mutual parenting scoring top marks. The fact that father routinely brings the toddler home to his mother at 7 p.m. on Sunday evenings should not mean that he cannot be brought home an hour earlier on one particular Sunday when his grandparents are to visit at 6 p.m. Only a desire to assert himself over the mother could make a father refuse to sacrifice that single hour to allow a visit that will be a treat for the child (and the grandparents). On another Sunday you may find yourself grumbling that 7 p.m. is not 7.10 – it isn't, of course, but the train may think that it is. Niggling insistence from either of you on the other parent sticking to the very letter of your arrangements will suggest that your parenting agreement has not been made willingly. It may need revision if it is to survive.

- In the long term, parents need always to be prepared to change arrangements, even arrangements they themselves are comfortable with, in order to make them comfortable for children. Children grow and change. Plans that suit a toddler may not suit him at all when he is four years old and starting school, while routines for a child newly at secondary school may need to change several times in the first year to accommodate her new independence and peer group.

Fathers and mothers

More and more fathers in intact couples play a very big part in children's daily lives, but very few – less than 10 per cent – become the resident parents after family breakdown. There are all kinds of reasons and composites of reasons why this is so. There are outdated but still commonplace conventions about divisions of family labour (Dad earns, Mum cares). There are down-to-earth practicalities that work against fathers taking equal shares in childcare commitments, such as men earning higher wages than women, meaning that a reduction in a father's working hours would cost a family more than a reduction in mother's. Similarly, paid paternity leave is twenty times shorter than maternity leave, while few employers are as accepting of a father's need for flexible working hours as they are of a mother's.

When parents separate, fathers often press for more contact with the children, and especially for overnight and weekend visits from them. Sometimes that is not because they actually want that extra time in charge of the children right now but because they are afraid that without it they will not be able to hold on to, or build, a close relationship with them after the separation. Research strongly suggests that this particular fear is groundless. The quality of contact – parent and child looking forward to seeing each other and having fun together – is even more important than its quantity, and for all but the youngest children, frequent communication, in all available forms – Facebook, Skype, Instagram, WhatsApp and texts, as well as phone, letters and postcards – thickens up the parent–child relationship between physical meetings.

RESEARCH

Daytime-Only Contact Does Not Reduce Attachment

Overnight care in early infancy does not appear to determine attachment security with the second parent. Warm, lively, attuned care-giving interactions between baby and the second parent appear to be what is central to the growth of attachment security in that relationship.

J.E. McIntosh, 'Special Considerations for Infants and Toddlers in Separation/Divorce', in R.E. Tremblay et al. (eds), *Encyclopedia on Early Childhood Development*, 2011 (online – http://www.child-encyclopedia.com

---

If arrangements are to build children's security and happiness after family breakdown, and especially their relationships with the non-resident parent, they have to take account of their lifestyle when you were together. For babies and toddlers especially, the prior relationship between parent and child is critical to good future planning. Although a lot of couples might have preferred it otherwise, many more mothers than fathers have been children's principal caregivers and attachment figures since they were born, and there are still many men, including truly loving fathers, who would be at a loss if left in sole charge of a baby or toddler for more than half a day.

FACTS

Fathers in Sole Charge

Recent American research shows that:

- One-third of fathers with working wives are a regular source of childcare for their children; this figure is higher in some non-white families.
- The number of dads regularly caring for their children increased from 26 per cent in 2002 to 32 per cent in 2010.
- Among fathers with pre-schoolers in 2010, 20 per cent were primary caregivers.
- The number of 'stay-at-home dads' increased by 50 per cent between 2003 and 2006.

American Psychological Association, 'The Changing Role of the Modern-day Father', 2013, www.apa.org/pi/families/ resources/changing-father.aspx

---

I'd trust him absolutely to do what's necessary for Liam, but I wouldn't trust him to do, or even to wonder, what's nice.

Mother of boy, aged eight months

Even with older children, a father who has not played much part in the practical details of their lives while the family was intact may struggle to keep them safe, secure and happy if he is suddenly left to cope alone. If you do not know the name of your child's best friend (this week) or teacher (this term), you'll have to climb to the top of a very steep learning curve before she is likely to be happy for you to pick her up from school.

> *I get muddled who's picking me up and where I'm going. My teacher tries to help. I think she has stuff about it written down. But I don't like it; don't like it that I don't know who to look for . . . that's why I was crying when he came yesterday. Not 'cause he was late or 'cause I didn't want to go with him, like my mum said, but 'cause I wasn't sure it was going to be him or who.*
>
> Girl, aged seven

You may, of course, always have been a wholeheartedly hands-on dad, but if not, don't despair. Once you are separated, you can learn what you did not feel the need to know before (Marilee and Miss Jeffreys), and children who love you will help. But the learning may take time. Both of you need to think honestly and realistically about what the sharing arrangements you are considering will actually be like for each of your children right now. Are they designed to help the children feel secure, or are they the arrangements that best suit you two or that strike you as 'fair'?

> *It was too far and cost too much for Daddy to come to see us for the day, so we had to go for weekends. Staying with him at the beginning was really sort of scary. He'd made a room for us which was OK-ish but no nightlight and he hadn't bought the kind of food Amelia ever eats (pork chops for supper and no biscuits) and he sort of didn't know how to look after her – or me come to that. He'd bathed Amelia and put her to bed lots of times, and so he did that OK, but then he came downstairs leaving her wide awake in a strange room and I had to take her*

for a wee and stay while she settled. Luckily I'd been allowed to babysit her sometimes since my birthday, so she was used to me taking care of her at night. But in the morning she was awake long before Dad (and long before I usually get up at weekends), so I had to wake up too and help her find clothes and get dressed and everything, and it just didn't feel like there was anybody but me in charge.

Girl, aged twelve, with a sister, aged three

Nobody should take it for granted that children will be better off almost entirely with the mother as 'primary caregiver'. Some fathers are not competent as carers when they are first in sole charge of young children, but neither are all mothers. Being a lone parent is extraordinarily different from being a partnered one, and even mothers who feel that their ex played little part in the children's lives before the separation sometimes have difficulty coping when they find themselves on their own with almost unrelieved and solitary childcare. Provided the father's motivation and intentions are good, that he is emotionally and physically available to the child, and that her safety with him is not in question, having her spend time with him may be valuable to all concerned, even if his parenting is unconventional.

Half-term with Daddy was kind of like camping. I slept on a mat and there was funny food and not much washing. It was really fun.

Girl, aged nine

Shared parenting usually means shared resources, of which money and housing are the most immediately important. It's commonplace for separating parents to quarrel over these, but before you get involved, or let your solicitors get you embroiled, take time to think about how much these adult-sounding issues can affect your children. Any arrangement that leaves one of you much poorer than the other can seriously jeopardise the poorer parent's opportunities for a loving, caring relationship with the children, and can even deprive children of contact with him or her.

Mothers' financial situations often nosedive after separation because their ex-husbands cannot or will not pay anything approaching adequate maintenance (see page 81) and their own earnings are inadequate or even threatened. Some women who continue to work full time after separation nevertheless find it impossible to run what was a family home on their single wage. And some women have to give up work once they are on their own because their hours, their earnings and the costs of childcare do not balance. Sudden household poverty can drain children's lives of accustomed pleasures. Even children who are old enough to understand that you are broke rather than mean are liable to resent your sudden refusal to let them go on school trips, carry on with out-of-school music or judo classes, or take their accustomed pocket money for granted.

Fathers – perhaps especially fathers who are trying to behave decently when their families break up – are just as likely to be left relatively poor, and where housing is concerned it is often fathers who suffer most. If the family was already struggling to meet mortgage and utility payments, divorce may be a final straw, and if the whole ex-family has to move out and is struggling to find alternative living accommodation, social services will probably help with some (basic) kind of housing for the mother and children but not for the father. He has become a single man whose welfare is no authority's responsibility and who may be left literally homeless.

FACTS

Shared Parenting and Poverty

In the UK, separation or divorce is a commonplace reason for employed men, especially men over 50, becoming homeless.

Ben Jackson, director of communications at Shelter said 'last year more than 27,000 householders became homeless as a direct result of relationship breakdown'.

T. Warnes and M. Crane, 2004, *Homelessness in the Over-fifties*, Report by the Economic and Social Research Council

---

If a separating couple is better off, the father may move out of the family home leaving the mother and children in it. However, unless he is notably well-off, it may be difficult, even impossible, to finance a second place to live where the children can comfortably visit. A room may be the best such a father can afford, and even if he moves into a flat the chances of both parental homes being equally child-friendly are very small. If your new 'home' is notably less nice than the family home you have left, your ex – or you yourself – may feel that it is not suitable for a baby or safe for a toddler, while older children will inevitably regret, even resent, moving between the two places, however eager they are to spend time with both people. If a child visits reluctantly, his time with you will do little to build your relationship and may actually make it more difficult to maintain.

> *I wanted equal time as a parent and my ex went along with it because it meant she was only a single mother part time. But the truth is that by the time I'd paid rent for the flat and maintenance to her for the kid, I was too broke to give Eric a great time. I couldn't afford lots of trips and days out; the flat was cramped, there wasn't a garden and he didn't have any*

*friends nearby. I knew he'd rather be at home with his mum
and his mates, and who could blame him?*

Father of boy, aged six

However mutual your parenting, you cannot stretch a tight budget further than it can reach, but you can resist scoring over each other financially or listening to lawyers telling you what you are entitled to instead of relying on your own sense of what will make the best of a bad job for the children.

PUTTING PARENTING PLANS INTO ACTION

The smooth running of your plans, especially contact between your children and their non-resident parent, depends on both of you being firmly committed to continuing contact at all costs. The most helpful stance either of you can adopt is as an active and proactive supporter of the relationship between each of your children and their mum and their dad, not only practically but also in the emotional sense of expecting and encouraging children to enjoy it. That's not always easy. Perhaps only someone who has seen their excited child off on an expedition with the other parent, so eager for the hello-hug that she forgets a goodbye one, can understand how difficult it can be. But since you could not all stay contentedly together as a family, this is the very best you can do, and in the long run of your child's growing up, it is worth any amount of effort.

However hard you are each trying, though, minor difficulties with contact arrangements are inevitable, especially at the beginning. Whether you are the resident or the contact parent, you are human and under tremendous stress. You can forget things (that swimming gear, again), be late for pick-up or drop-off, seem grumpy or disapproving of the other parent, or strain your parenting plan by allowing or encouraging a child to behave in ways the other parent has vetoed (too much TV). The great majority of contact problems are of this kind; niggling disagreements that are commonplace within most intact marriages and, given mutual goodwill, easily overlooked or dealt with by compromise. It is when goodwill is lacking that difficulties escalate into conflicts that can threaten contact itself.

> *I love my time with the kids. I get through the working week for those weekends with them. But I dread picking them up and taking them back 'cause it seems I can't do anything right. I try very hard not to be late, but with the trains, it can happen, and you should hear him if I'm early . . . I try to do things with the boys that he'll approve of like swimming, but last time we did that it turned out that Felix had had an ear infection and wasn't supposed to go in the water. He hadn't told me, had he? But that didn't stop him calling me irresponsible in front of them both. As for food: you'd never think I'd been the one who shopped and cooked for them for seven years. He quizzes me about what they've had so I feel I should be writing out menus. It can't really be that he doesn't trust me: I'm a good mum and always have been, so the truth is he doesn't want me to have them; maybe hopes I'll drop out.*
>
> Mother of two boys, aged eight and nine

When contact is difficult to arrange so that children are often kept on tenterhooks and sometimes disappointed, or if visits are more or less miserable and children resist them, it's all too easy for one or both parents to decide that the children would be better off without contact, or simply to let it dwindle and lapse. Easy, but wrong. A very large body of research shows that there are no circumstances, not even extremes, such as a parent being in prison for something horrible, in which it is better for a child if a parent is airbrushed out of his life. There are many different types of contact. If one really cannot be made to work, try another.

RESEARCH

Drifting Away from Contact with Absent Parents

In an American sample of more than 11,000 children, almost a quarter of separated fathers started with frequent contact, which gradually dwindled to nothing.

High levels of father involvement were more likely when children were older at the time of separation and were more likely to be maintained when fathers and mothers lived close to each other.

Separated mothers were more likely to be highly involved with their children and much less likely to drift out of contact.

From *Children of the National Longitudinal Survey* 20, 2002;
J.E. Cheadle, P. Amato and V. King, 'Patterns of Non-residential
Father Contact', Demography 47 (1), 2010

OVERNIGHT STAYS – AGES AND CIRCUMSTANCES

Most parenting plans include overnight stays with the non-resident parent (usually the father), often one or two weekend nights at a time and usually some half-term or holiday nights also. It is overnight contact that causes most problems between, and for, parents. When it works well there are major advantages over day visits: notably, that the child has the opportunity to 'live with' the contact parent; that the two of them have a base rather than having to spend their time together visiting relatives or friends, making expeditions or wandering aimlessly around the park; and that the contact parent cares for the child through every minute of the day and night and every aspect of his or her way of being.

Daddy wears glasses in the night and contact lenses in the day!
I saw him put them in . . .

Girl aged four

However, overnights don't always work well. Mothers often find them hard to bear and therefore difficult to support, while fathers who are in poor accommodation or who work long and inflexible hours may not be able to provide appropriate care. Overnight stays with the non-resident parent are particularly likely to be inappropriate for a baby or toddler who is not accustomed to being away from mother or cared for by father.

A considerable amount of research into the question of overnights with non-resident parents for these youngest children has been carried out. Some of the best of it is summarised below.

RESEARCH

Overnight Care for Children of Parents Living Apart: Part 1

A think-tank convened by the US Association of Family and Conciliation Courts (AFCC) ('Closing the Gap: Research, Policy, Practice, and Shared Parenting') and the two-part paper that followed it have advanced research in this contentious area. An important area of consensus is that post-divorce care arrangements should take account of both early attachment formation and joint parental involvement rather than focusing on one or the other.

There are five studies comparing the outcomes for very young children of different patterns of shared care, including

---

overnights with the non-resident parent. Consensus was reached that: 'The small group of relevant studies to date substantiates caution about high frequency overnight time schedules in the 0–3 year period, particularly when the child's security with a parent is unformed, or parents cannot agree on how to share care of the child . . . [but] cautions against any overnight care in the first three years have not been supported.

M.K. Pruett, J.E. McIntosh and J.B. Kelly, 'Parental Separation and Overnight Care of Young Children, Part I: Consensus through Theoretical and Empirical Integration', *Family Court Review* 52 (2) (2014), pp. 240–55

Overnight Care for Children of Parents Living Apart – Part 2: Putting Theory into Practice

This companion piece to Part I is a guide to decision making about infant overnight care, principally directed to the family court community but useful also to parents. AFCC research emphasises that 'parenting orders or plans for children 0–3 years should foster both developmental security and the health of each parent–child relationship, now and into the future', and charts recommended frequencies of overnights from 'rare or no overnights' through one to four per month and five-plus per month against a list of considerations. 'Rare or no overnights' should be considered if a child:

- Is not safe with both parents or the parents with each other.
- Does not have an established trusting relationship of at least six months with the non-resident parent.
- Has needs to which the parent is not sensitive.
- Has special needs (including continuing breast-feeding) that are not supported in proposed arrangements.

- Over three to four weeks shows signs of stress such as irritability, excessive clinging on separation, frequent crying, aggressive or self-harming behaviour, regression in established behaviours such as toileting, low persistence in play and learning.
- Has parents who live an unmanageable distance apart.
- Has a parent who cannot personally care for the child overnight but must use childcare.

J.E. McIntosh, M.K. Pruett and J.B. Kelly, 'Parental
Separation and Overnight Care of Young Children, Part II:
Putting Theory into Practice', *Family Court Review* 52 (2) (2014),
pp. 256–62

Sleepovers for babies and toddlers

Staying overnight with the contact parent does not only mean that the child has to go to and settle in an unaccustomed place but also, of course, that he must leave the resident parent and the home set-up in order to do so. The younger the child, the more likely it is that the leaving element – leaving Mum and home – will be stressful. As suggested earlier, overnight stays for babies and toddlers should not be taken for granted (see page 31). They may work well for all concerned if both parents were involved in his care while the family was intact and he is confidently attached to both, and they may be helpful overall if the resident parent badly needs respite, but generally speaking, regular and frequent nights away should usually wait until a child is three years old.

If you do decide to include overnight stays with the non-resident parent in your parenting plan for a baby or toddler, it may be quite difficult to be sure how this is affecting him; you and his father will both need to put yourself in his small shoes in order to understand. A one- or two-year-old who is going for an overnight stay is not old enough to understand the plan or to anticipate how long he will be away, so although he may well be distressed at the point of separation from you, he'll be no more distressed than if he was going to Dad for the afternoon. Once that mini-parting is over, he is misleadingly likely to appear to 'settle' with the less familiar parent in the new place, and it is only when he is returned home and reunited with you that the full extent of any upset will become clear. It is the mother's relationship with the child that is vulnerable to too-early separations, and you are the one who will bear the brunt of his clingy and unsettled behaviour.

RESEARCH

Some Links between Frequent Overnights and Behavioural Problems in Babies and Toddlers

- Babies and toddlers under two years of age who spent one or more nights a week with a non-resident parent were more irritable than children who were primarily in the care of one parent, and they also kept a closer watch on the whereabouts of the primary caregiver than babies with no overnight time.
- Children aged two to three years who spent five or more nights a fortnight with a non-resident parent showed significantly lower levels of persistence with routine tasks, with learning and in sociable play than children who were primarily or entirely in the care of one parent in one place.
- The attachment distress of regularly separated toddlers could be seen in their relationships with the resident parent. Some became very upset, crying or clinging to the parent; others became aggressive, hitting, biting or kicking. A few developed eating problems such as food refusal or gagging.

> • No ill-effects of being 'time-shared' between parents were evident in children past their fourth birthdays.
>
> J.E. McIntosh *et al.*, *Post-Separation Parenting Arrangements and Developmental Outcomes for Infants and Children*, Collected Reports for the Australian Government, Attorney General's Department, 2013

The research information noted in the boxes above was gathered for very large groups of children from many different families. It does not mean that staying with Dad overnight should be ruled out for your particular baby or toddler, or that it will certainly be appropriate for your individual three-year-old. You, your children and your environments are all unique. The mix of your and your ex's relationships, temperaments, needs and circumstances may be a recipe that makes any contact arrangement stressful for a very young child or that makes it supportive. You may find helpful an online education program specifically for separated parents, called Young Children in Divorce and Separation (YCIDS).

Young Children in Divorce and Separation (YCIDS): An Online Programme for Parents

YCIDS is a ninety-minute online education programme for separated parents of very young children. YCIDS simplifies complex research, supporting parents to better understand early development, and to better manage co-parenting of very young children, between two homes. Parents can complete it at home, or as part of a divorce mediation or court process.

Source: http://www.familytransitions.com.au

What the research information does make clear is that if you are working out arrangements for contact between the parent who is non-resident and a baby, toddler or pre-school child, you need to consider questions such as the following very carefully before you settle on frequent overnight stays:

- What is the child's existing relationship with the non-resident parent (probably her father)? Leaving you in order to stay with Daddy overnight is unlikely to be upsetting if he was her primary or equal caregiver before the separation, or if he is entirely accustomed to caring for her by night and day and she demonstrates her attachment to him by readily turning to him when she needs reassurance or comfort. However, if hands-on parenting of this child will be more or less new to them both, overnights with the father should ideally wait until some months of daytime contact have helped them to build a relationship.
- Can the child's father provide constant personal care while she is with him? If he will need to go out to work or to socialise, and plans to employ a babysitter, he may not be in a position to have such a young child to stay with him on his own. However, if the child has a caregiver at home, a nanny, au pair or babysitter, having that person go with her to the father's home overnight may solve that problem, as well as giving him some support in caring for her.
- Are there older siblings who will regularly and frequently stay overnight with their father? If so, it may be difficult to arrange separate daytime contact for the youngest child and seem better for everyone if all the children go together.
- The more frequent and the longer are overnight stays, the more stress they tend to put on a child. Consider one night at a time rather than two, and on alternate weekends rather than every week, with daytime contact in between.

- Do you, as resident parent, probably the mother, have urgent practical reasons for wanting this child to stay away from home for regular overnights? If you have mental or physical health problems or are suffering from stress or exhaustion, overnight breaks can help you to maintain the quality of your parenting. However, if separating from you to stay with her father is, in the event, unmanageably stressful for the child, any respite her absence might give you will be lost because it is on her return home and in her relationship with you that her anxious, unsettled, clingy or aggressive behaviour will show itself.

Such changes in behaviour need to be taken seriously, as they may sometimes reflect real and lasting disturbance to a child's development rather than a temporary 'upset'. It is enormously important that all children, even the youngest, see the contact parent regularly, but how that is arranged is equally important.

Overnight visits for older children

Although it would be idiotic to suggest that every child under four is better off without overnight contact but then becomes ready for it on his fourth birthday, these research studies do strongly suggest that staying away overnight becomes less difficult at around that age.

RESEARCH

Overnight Visits for Four- and Five-Year-Olds

Most of the variation between overnight care groups among four- to five-year-olds with separated parents was accounted for by factors other than overnight care patterns, with

---

> particular emphasis on the impact of inter-parental conflict
> and lack of warmth in parenting on children's self-regulating
> capacities at this stage.
>
> J.E. McIntosh *et al.*, *Post-Separation Parenting Arrangements and*
> *Developmental Outcomes for Infants and Children*,
> Collected Reports for the Australian Government, Attorney
> General's Department, 2010

School-aged children are far less likely to find leaving you for a night or two highly stressful in itself. Their attachment is developed, and hopefully secure, and their ability to understand plans and antici-pate reunion is dawning if not yet complete. Furthermore, many of them are accustomed to occasional sleepovers with friends or grandparents, which means not only that they are accustomed to being away from you but also that they are used to sleeping in a dif-ferent bed in another house. For these older children, what matters most of all is that spending time with their father, and staying over-night with him, is a pleasure, in prospect and in fact. Of course this mostly depends on the relationship between them and on issues dealt with earlier, such as whether or not the child will be with sib-lings and where and how the contact parent lives. However, there are other points that may be helpful to smooth-running contact that is satisfactory for the child, however difficult it may be for one or both parents.

- Being not only allowed but also encouraged to look forward to their times with the non-resident parent. You can easily turn pleasurable anticipation into guilt by denigrating the father or bemoaning your loneliness when the child is away.
- Feeling able to talk to one parent about time spent with the other but never being pressured to do so or asked to carry messages between the two.

- Having arrangements with a balanced mixture of regularity and flexibility. A child will not look forward to a weekend with Dad if she will be missing her best friend's birthday party.
- Having the contact parent's full-time presence and plenty of attention. Arriving for the weekend to find that Dad has to work on Saturday is a put-down, whatever care he has arranged to cover his absence. Equally, the child wants to spend time with his father, not with his father's friends or his lover, so extra adults are usually unwelcome.
- Something fun to do with the parent. Overnight visits work best when the child gets to do something with Dad that he really enjoys and doesn't get to do regularly otherwise:

It's since I started going to my dad's at weekends that I've really started swimming. We go to a great big pool and he comes in with me to swim and then I get a swimming lesson. Last week the teacher said I'm doing well and this week I'm moving up a group.

Boy, aged nine

- Being able to keep in contact with home life during contact visits if he or she wishes. Children should be free to phone or text the other parent and to do so privately if they want to. For older children, in particular, contact with friends may be overwhelmingly import-ant. A child who texts or goes on Facebook from home should not need special permission to do so when with the other parent.
- With school the next morning, Sunday evenings are often rushed and stressful, even when children have been at home all week-end. Having been away, combined with the transition from one parent to another, can make things worse. To keep Sundays calm, children need to feel comfortable fulfilling school commitments during weekend visits. There must be time, encouragement and a suitable place to do homework or revise for a test.

Teenagers often find regular weekend contact very difficult, even if parents allow some flexibility. Both of you need to accept that:

- The young person's peer group probably matters more to her than either parent (at least at a conscious level). She wants to be where her friends will – or can – be. Unless the parents live in the same community, she is not likely to want to go away very often.
- Most young people are very bad at making plans in advance. Your teenager will not be able to choose which weekends he can be away without missing anything that matters to him because he will not know what he is doing, when. And it is useless to pressure him to decide because he has no idea what his friends will be doing when, either. The chances are that none of them will be doing anything adults recognise as special (and can therefore be put in a diary). What they will be doing is hanging out.
- If the father's area or home offers something interesting (such as proximity to an important football stadium or a seaside location), encouraging the teenager to invite friends to come with her may help to keep up her enthusiasm for weekends with her father. She may not accept, though. However much her father has to offer, she may not want to mix friends from one home and parent with the other.
- The only important criterion of good contact arrangements is that the child and her father spend enjoyable time together. If your teenager no longer enjoys regular weekends or even resents the pressure to go on with them, her father might offer to meet up with her for supper and a movie in her home area, or to rendezvous in the nearest town. Any such suggestion will make it clear that Dad is eager to see her on whatever terms she finds comfortable.

DAYTIME CONTACT

Seeing the non-resident parent during the day rather than over-night suits a lot of children, especially the very young, and if parents live close to each other and their parenting is at least polite if not mutual, daytime contact is so easy that overnight or weekend visiting that is genuinely for everyone's pleasure often develops out of it.

> We like having sleepovers with our dad, don't we Tom? But you always have to go home in the middle of the night, don't you? And then I have to go too.
>
> Twin girl and boy, aged four

As those children grew older, they began to choose which house-hold they would be in on any particular day, and by the time they left primary school they could (and often did) walk between the two houses. They had a bedroom as well as a parent in each.

From children's points of view, that is an ideal to aspire to, but it is not one that many couples will achieve because living close together with a lot of popping in and out going on is not what most people who are separating or divorcing want. Geography is crucial, though. If parents both want the children to see both of them, even if they don't want to see each other, it is living nearby that will make it possible.

If the two of you live a long way apart, visits will cost a lot of money – in fares or fuel – and time, and a few hours with the child may not seem enough to make the non-resident parent's journey worthwhile for him or the resultant freedom worthwhile for you. Furthermore, it is really difficult to have a fun time with a child without a base to go to. Football in the park is fine while the sun shines and the child's energy runs high, but what if it pours with rain and he is tired? Under those circumstances 'ordinary' families go home and a young child will not fully understand why Dad and he cannot. Whether you have decided to stick with daytime contact because your child is too young for sleeping away or because the father's accommodation isn't suitable for overnight stays, this is a fragile kind of contact, which all too often deteriorates and then fades away.

> *I regret the contact now. I wish I'd broken it completely. I don't think he'd have bothered taking me to court if I'd said no. I thought the kids needed a link with him – and maybe they do – but their contact with him has been so erratic that they've never known if he was coming or not and that's probably been more damaging than if they'd just never seen him.*
> Mother of three children, separated for two years

Since nothing apart from losing both parents is more damaging to a child than having one parent vanish out of her life, it is worth considering some ways of making daytime contact with a parent who doesn't live nearby easier and more lasting:

- Could you, the resident parent, allow your ex to use your and the child's own home as a base for visits? If you don't want to see your ex, you could go out for the afternoon. If you can't bear the idea of him being in the house alone as if it was still his, would your mother or a friend agree to be there?
- If your home is completely out of bounds, is there a relative or friend whom you trust and the child knows and likes who would let them meet in her house?
- Does the child already spend occasional nights with grandparents or other relatives who live locally? If so, could father visit the child there?
- Is there an indoor activity centre that your child enjoys to which you could drive her to meet and spend time with her father, who would then bring her home?

- Failing anything more personal, is there a contact centre to which you could drive the child to meet up with her father?

For older children and teenagers, daytime visits between longer weekends or holidays may be the more valuable because of the effort they cost the contact parent. The children will realise that if Dad takes all that trouble to get to the school play or the GCSE subject-choice evening or an important cricket match, he really cares about their lives.

Sometimes these visits can take place without the parents meeting each other: a school play often has two or three performances, and parents could therefore go separately. A concert is a one-off, though, and so is a sports event or a school consultation, so although attending such functions together may not be something you discussed when you were first making parenting plans, it is an issue that eventually needs to be addressed. Teenage or student accomplishments often involve public performance or acknowledgement. Is one of you always going to miss the days when your child most wants you to be proud of him – such as school prize-giving or university degree day? And what about the opposite kind of day when he needs a parent's presence and support: will only one of you answer a call to the police station or even A&E?

SUPERVISED CONTACT

Sometimes a mother really does not want her children to see their father at all, even for brief daytime visits. Her ex cannot insist on seeing the children against her wishes, but neither can she prevent him just because that is what she would prefer. A father may be so intimidated by an angry ex that he backs off and the children are deprived of contact with him, but if a solicitor, mediator or CAFCASS officer is involved, it will become clear to the mother that she really cannot keep the children from seeing their father without a reason to which the family court would pay attention.

If two parents cannot sort the question of father's access out between them, the matter should go to court quickly so that as little time as possible elapses before regular contact with the child is established or re-established. Although he may not realise it, the father can apply for a Child Arrangements Order (see p. 89). Once an application has been made, parents are in the court's hands. The court will make an order if it thinks that this is in the child's best interests, but it may not be the order either one of the parents expected or would have chosen. Child protection is the court's priority, so the mother's concerns will be carefully listened to; but the court recognises the importance to children of contact with both parents and will therefore try to balance the two. Often neither parent is satisfied by what is ordered. Most mothers are indignant if any contact is ordered against their expressed wishes, and most fathers find any compulsory limits or supervision of their time with the children deeply insulting. A solution that both parents work out between themselves might be far more satisfactory.

CONTACT FROM A DISTANCE

In this era of increasingly sophisticated communications, parents and children can stay in touch with each other even when they cannot spend time together, and it's important to realise how much this can help their relationships, even when practical circumstances are against them. Regular and frequent contact with the non-resident parent assures children that although he is no longer physically present in their home, their father is still their father and as loving, interested and concerned for them as ever. And when children are with the father, they similarly need to know that although they are away from their mother, she is still there for them. However desperately an absent parent misses being with a child in person – talking and listening, hugging and holding hands, playing games and washing faces – contact in words and pictures is a lot better than nothing. Most children love getting mail and will be thrilled with letters or picture postcards. A supply of ready-addressed and -stamped cards makes it easy for a child to reply.

Phones are obvious channels of communication but sometimes expensive – especially if you are on different continents – and not always very comfortable for children under about five, who love to answer but find it difficult to listen to what the caller is saying and then reply. If your child is comfortable using a phone, you might give him a pay-as-you-go mobile rather earlier than you would have done if the family had stayed intact, so that he knows he can call you to make arrangements or to chat, and do so privately. Some children find it difficult to talk in front of Mum or in front of siblings. Older children are usually inseparable from their mobiles, which means that you can reach out to them at almost any time. Being phoned is disruptive, though. The solution is texting, and today's children become exceedingly competent at sending and reading texts at a surprisingly early age.

If there is a computer available and the resident parent will help, videophone services, such as Skype, offer richer contact possibilities for all ages than an ordinary phone, and calls are free however far apart you are and however long they last. Being able to see each other is especially valuable to a very young child because it will help her to hang on to a clear image of you over months of separation.

Emails are also invaluable, not only for words but for sharing photos. Whether the child uses a laptop, a smartphone or a tablet, it will probably be worth getting her an email address of her own.

Social networking sites such as Facebook keep millions of people in touch with each other, but children cannot use them until they are thirteen years old, and even then may not want a parent potentially mixed up with their peers. If your child has a smartphone, he can use FaceTime or take pictures of things he wants to show you, email them to you, and get an immediate voice or voicemail reaction. A supply of ready-addressed and -stamped cards makes it easy for a child to reply.

CHAPTER 8

WHEN CONTACT FAILS

Everybody who is professionally involved with parents who are separating – such as researchers, social workers, solicitors and the family courts – believes that it is in children's best interests to be in contact with both parents: the non-resident parent as well as the parent they live with; and that it is parents' responsibility to make sure that they are. This book goes somewhat further. What it calls 'separating better' is largely concerned with the relationships parents can make with each other, and the parenting plans they can put in place to ensure not just that the children stay in contact with them both but that they both go on being mother or father to them.

Problems around contact are inevitable, and commonplace ones that contribute to 'separating worse' have been dealt with in earlier chapters. But the ultimate problem, fortunately not at all commonplace, is not just difficulty around contact between child and non-resident parent but absolute refusal of it.

WILLING PARENT, RELUCTANT CHILD

In law, contact with both parents is a child's right; contact with a child is not a parent's right. The welfare and best interests of a child are the most important of a court's considerations, and while the wishes and feelings of children are also acknowledged, that doesn't mean that children can choose whether to have contact with a parent or not. How much, if any, notice a court takes of children's wishes depends on their age and assumed level of understanding. There is no set age at which a child's views will be taken into account by a court, but the wishes of older children – especially teenagers – may be taken more seriously than those of younger ones. In the eyes of some resident parents, though, they are not taken seriously enough.

She dreads seeing him. Really dreads going to that centre place and sitting and talking to him. But still she has to go every three weeks and I have to take her. If I didn't I'd be in breach of a court order. They could even send me to prison, I think.

Mother of girl, aged fourteen

Courts take the view that unless there is an officially recognised child protection issue, it is parents' responsibility to make their child take part in contact whatever the child's feelings about the matter.

No child is old enough to make a decision about contact if that means choosing which of his parents he prefers to live with or how much time he wants to spend with the other. No child should even be asked to make such an agonising choice, especially knowing that the sense of what he says will be shared with both parents. But no child who can speak fluently is too young to express his feelings about seeing the non-resident parent, and these should certainly be heard – as they are when a full assessment of the family dynamics and patterns of attachment are made by 'expert witnesses' – and fed into the court's adult decision making. Unfortunately, such assessments add to the duration and costs of divorce cases and are not always ordered, or carried out by relevantly trained professionals.

Many parents say that when their child resisted seeing the parent she didn't live with, they found themselves in double trouble. When contact had been ordered by the court, or had been arranged in mediation and would come to court if it didn't work out, they were held responsible for making it happen, and if it didn't happen they were in trouble. Trying to convince a mediator or CAFCASS worker that she had done her best to get the child to contact but the child really refuses to go does not get the resident parent off the hook. On the contrary, it may be assumed that if a child completely rejects contact with the other parent it must be because the resident parent has put her off.

The Family Justice Council has recently recommended that young people should participate more fully in the court process by being included in any mediation and, for example, writing to the judge or even seeing him. But many professionals in divorce work are against this.

QUOTES

When Did You Last See Your Father?

'Children often make allegations about their parents which are not credible; children can feel unable to express their view or may even be unable to form their own view of a matter, so their expressed wishes and feelings may be misleading.

'A child may express the view that s/he does not wish to see their parent; this view may reflect a negative view of the non-resident parent by the parent with day-to-day care which may be reinforced by that parent's immediate circle of family and friends. Sometimes other professionals are also enlisted by the resident parent, who may for example tell a GP or school that the child suffers from stomach cramps, headaches or bedwetting prior to visits with the other parent.'

Ian Kirkland Weir, Hertfordshire Family Forum, Neves Solicitors LLP, 8 July 2013

Contact with a non-resident parent works best when child and parent look forward to seeing each other and enjoy being together. If that has never been the case for your family, or if it was the case for a while but the child has now begun to protest about visits and says that he doesn't want to go, don't let the situation drag on. The more time passes since child and parent spent time together, the more reluctant the child will probably become. There are many reasons why children refuse contact, and it's important to come to understand, as quickly as possible, what kind of problem is putting your child off. Is it to do with what he feels about the other parent or is it to do with what he feels about you (and leaving you)? Or is the problem something specific about the circumstances of his visits?

- Encourage your child to tell you about what he feels about seeing the other parent. Even a four-year-old may be able to explain why he doesn't want to talk to him or visit. Sometimes, unwillingness to spend time with the other parent hinges on specific things that can be changed and put right, such as always having to share the visit with the parent's future partner or not being allowed a night-light.
- Try not to let the child pick up on your own thoughts or feelings about the man who is your ex-partner but his current-and-forever dad. As we have seen, you don't have to intend to alienate a child to do so. If you are furiously angry and upset with your ex, it is really difficult for a child who lives with you and loves you to put your feelings aside and look forward to seeing and loving him. If you think the child is old enough to understand, it may be helpful to spell out for him the difference between his father's partnership with you (which has failed and made you furious) and his parenting of the child, which hasn't failed and makes you happy.
- Realise that whether he shows it in conventional ways or not, your child is experiencing real grief at the loss not only of the parent

who doesn't live with him any more but also of the pair of you as he knew you. However hard you try, neither of you is the same parent (or the same person) as you were before the family broke up, and his rejection of the contact arranged for him may be part of a refusal to accept what feels to him so much of a second best.

- Understand that an agony of conflict and split loyalty is inevitable for your child. He loves you both, yet every sign of love for one feels like disloyalty to the other. He may be unable to feel comfortable with the other parent because visits inevitably involve hugs, and hugs make him feel guilty.

- Recognise that your child's reactions to contact with the other parent are almost certainly linked to the relationship between the two of you. The more mutual your parenting (see p. 102) the less likely it is that a child will refuse contact. Conversely, the fact that your child is refusing contact suggests that the two of you are not on good terms or perhaps are not on terms at all. Do try to keep (or reinstate) some kind of communication with your ex so that the two of you can discuss what the real problem is and what is to be done.

Reasons for children refusing contact

If your child's complete refusal of contact with the non-resident parent shows up before a visit has even begun, it may be that the very beginning is most of the problem. Maybe he would be perfectly fine once he and his father got away together. But if they don't get away together, you don't know; you can only find out if you can deal with the handover.

Handover times are often the most difficult parts of contact visits for younger children, and even older children (who are expected to go rather than be handed over) sometimes find the actual transition from one parent to the other very conflictual, so some degree of difficulty is commonplace. As we have seen, there are many ways you can help, from making the handover quick and smooth with no lingering goodbyes to dropping off or collecting a child from a neutral place such as school or a relative's house. However, if extreme problems with handover are part of a child's attempt to refuse contact altogether, such simple measures are unlikely to solve them.

A young child may adamantly refuse to leave you, clinging to your leg or your skirt and keeping his head buried so as not to see his father. If he is small enough he could be (and some children are) literally 'handed over', screaming and struggling. That is not a good way to make a child feel that leaving Mum is safe and going with Dad is fun. In fact a child who is physically forced into handover is likely to remember his fear and frustration rather than his eventual enjoyment of the visit, and anticipate them next time a visit is proposed. An older child may show his unhappiness and anger by meeting insistence that he go with his father with passive resistance. If a child who is too big to be moved by force is prepared to cast himself to the ground like a toddler, he may win, at least for the moment. More often, though, a teenager will refuse contact by locking himself in his room and refusing to appear for the intended handover. Occasionally, an older child or teenager who is ambivalent about both parents and the contact they have arranged for him will turn the tables on them by going with his father, as planned, and then refusing to return home at the end of a visit.

Problems at handover obviously affect (and are horrible for) you both. Don't try to sort them out in front of the child. If this is the first time it's come up and you haven't planned how to cope, do whatever seems best at the time, but arrange to talk about it later. If you are not on direct telephoning terms you'll need to enlist whoever has helped you in mediation or specifically in making access arrangements. It is urgent. If you allow visits to go on starting with hysterical distress, or allow the distress to put an end to the visits, the relationship between father and child can only get worse, and there is a real risk of it petering out altogether in the face of the child's rejection and the father's repeated hurt and humiliation.

Secret fears

Sometimes a child has an actual reason for refusing contact, which she is unwilling or unable to tell you about. Reasons sometimes include previous physical, sexual or emotional abuse, or the child having felt frighteningly unsafe during earlier contact.

> *My little sister and I had to spend three weeks of the summer*
> *holidays with our father. He never actually did anything*
> *wrong but I was always terrified that he would. Like if I forgot*
> *something (there was a gate I always forgot to shut) he'd say,*
> *'What shall I do? Shall I spank you?' Or when I came out*
> *of the bath (the bathroom was downstairs) in pyjamas he'd*
> *say, 'There's my pretty girl; come and give a lonely man a big*
> *cuddle.' I know it sounds harmless but it wasn't. But how could*
> *I have explained to my mum?*
>
> Adult woman looking back to when she was eleven

No child should be compelled into contact that frightens her. If this seems to be the case, an expert assessment of each family member in relation to the others needs to be carried out so as to establish not only the facts but also the feelings of all concerned. Does the other parent press for regular visits with the child because he loves and misses her, or is his motive concerned with keeping control over you? Does the child really hate his father as he says, or does he think you will be pleased if he says that? Talk to a solicitor or to CAFCASS about assessment and the possibility of a subsequent application to the court for an order restricting contact.

Separation anxiety

Much the commonest reason for serious problems over contact is separation anxiety, which is global rather than specific and is not due to any inappropriate behaviour by the parent. Most babies and toddlers are liable to get anxious when they are parted from the parent they are most attached to. Contact with the non-resident parent (usually Dad) almost always means leaving Mum and home. Crying, clinging and tantrums are normal reactions to separation, from late in the first year until around four years old, but the intensity and timing vary widely from child to child. Some children will go on getting anxious about leaving you (or having you leave them) all through the primary school years. That's what those Sunday night blues or Monday morning tummy aches are about.

In intact families and under ordinary circumstances, separation anxiety becomes less frequent and less intense as the child grows up. In the meantime, you can do a lot to ease it by combining being understanding and sympathetic with your child's anxious feelings with being firm and clear that what is being asked of him is safe and that he should do it.

For a while he got so upset about school and I got so upset at having to leave him crying in his classroom that I wondered if I should let him have a break at home with me. But children do have to go to school, don't they? It seemed better that he should face that . . . By half-term he only cried on Monday mornings and by the next term he didn't cry at all!

Mother of boy, aged six

Some children's separation anxiety doesn't just go away and stay away, though, but lasts for months or years and is so severe that it gets in the way of all the child's normal activities, developing into what many health professionals call separation anxiety disorder. Developmentally normal separation anxiety and separation anxiety disorder share many signs and symptoms, but they differ in the intensity of your child's fears and how little it takes to touch them off. If your child is moving into separation anxiety disorder, being left alone in bed while you go downstairs may cause her panic, and just the thought of leaving the house without you may be enough to upset her.

Separation anxiety is about a child feeling unsafe. In the very early years, your child's attachment to you means that she feels unsafe whenever you aren't there or available to her if she needs you. Later on, and if the more extreme separation anxiety disorder develops, it will be because something has thrown the child off balance; made her feel threatened and unable to cope, or to manage herself and her world, and therefore to feel extra-dependent on you to do it for her.

Many separate life-events can play a part in increasing normal separation anxiety or tipping a susceptible child towards separation anxiety disorder. But other than the death of a parent, nothing is more likely to bring those separate events together than parental separation.

When you separate, your child may face:

- loss of a parent;
- loss of other love-objects such as caregivers or pets;
- changes in her environment such as a new house, school or day-care nursery;
- the stress associated with all the above changes;
- your anxiety and distress, which she will sense and which will feed her own.

If your child's separation anxiety is within ordinary limits except that it is inappropriate to his age, there is a lot you can do to help him to feel safer, especially if the other parent will play his part.

- Practise separation. Make contact visits very brief at first, then gradually extend them as the child becomes more positive (or less anxious) about leaving Mum to go with Dad.
- For babies and toddlers, schedule contact visits for times of day

when the child is at his most calm and cheerful – often in the second half of the afternoon after lunch and a nap.

- Have a special 'goodbye' ritual that you use whenever the child is separated from you and which he will therefore find reassuring when he leaves you to go with the other parent. Don't spin the leave-taking out though. Keep it as brief as a hug, a kiss on the nose and a few words such as 'Love you. See you soon. Have fun.'

- Try to have the separation take place in familiar surroundings. If contact cannot start from home without raising your stress-level intolerably, try making the handover in another neutral, familiar place such as a grandparent's home.

- When a small child leaves, make sure he takes a familiar and beloved toy or cuddly with him (but make sure the other parent realises it is important and doesn't let it get lost during the outing).

- However upset the child is, try not to give in and let him stay at home with you after all. He needs to know that you and the other parent are both confident that he will be OK and have a good time without you.

Separation anxiety disorder

The above tips may do something to help the child with separation anxiety disorder and will certainly do no harm. But it is important to realise how much more serious separation anxiety disorder is than separation anxiety.

Your child will feel constantly worried – every hour of every day – in case something happens that leads to him being separated from you, and will be acutely fearful when one does. The fear that overwhelms him will probably be one or more of the following:

- Fear that if he goes away, something terrible will happen to someone he loves; most commonly, that terrible harm (an accident, an illness, a murder, insanity) will come to you while he is gone. When children cannot leave home to go to school, it is not entirely school they fear but what may happen to a parent in their absence.

Every day, coming home on the bus, I'd see myself going in by the kitchen door and Mummy being there but quite mad so she didn't recognise me.

Grandmother recalls herself, aged seven

- Worry that once he is separated from you, something – such as getting lost or being kidnapped – will happen to make the separation permanent.
- Nightmares about being taken away from you or about losing you in a forest or watching you vanish into the sea.

Because of these fears, a child with separation anxiety disorder may:

- Refuse to go anywhere without you. That means that he not only refuses planned contact with the other parent but also school and play dates with friends.
- Be extremely reluctant to be left alone in bed and terrified to go to sleep.
- Suffer from a range of psychosomatic complaints such as headaches and tummy aches.
- Prefer to be within touch or sight of you all the time, such that, if he is small, he may literally cling on to you as you move around and if he is older he may shadow you from room to room, even waiting for you outside the bathroom like a toddler.

Helping the child with separation anxiety disorder

Anything you can do to make your child feel safer in herself, her life, her home and her relationships can help. Even if you cannot completely solve the problem, your understanding and sympathy can only make things better.

- Find out all you can about separation anxiety disorder and what your child is suffering, so that it is clear to her that you understand. Older children in particular recognise that their fears are fantastical and are afraid of not being taken seriously.
- Listen carefully to anything your child will tell you about her feelings. Encourage her to talk; there's nothing to be gained by trying not to think about it.
- Remind the child – gently – that despite all that worry, he or she survived the last separation and all the separations before it.
- Anticipate times that are likely to cause separation difficulty and try different ways of helping. If your child finds it easier to leave you at home than at the school gate, get a friend to take her to school instead of you and get your ex to start contact visits from the friend's home.
- Provide as consistent a daily pattern at home as you can. Don't underestimate the importance of predictability for children with separation anxiety problems. If the contact arrangements are going to change or a visitor is coming to stay, discuss it with your child ahead of time. During the months when anxiety is acute, try not to accept work or social commitments at such short notice that the child unexpectedly finds that you are not at home.
- Be careful not to let your child's anxiety buy endless indulgence. She needs your sympathy but she needs limits too. Let her know that although you understand her feelings about going to bed, to school or on contact visits, she does have to go, and remind her how well she managed last time.
- Offering the child choices or elements of control in an activity or interaction with an adult may help him or her to feel safer and more comfortable. She has to go to her Saturday music class: how

would she prefer to manage the journey and being there without you?

You know what makes a really big, huge difference? Knowing that Mum will be there to meet me when school or something else I have to do without her finishes. Just thinking about her waiting at the gate really helps. I know it's babyish being met, but she says 'better met than absent'!

Girl, aged ten

Your own patience and know-how can certainly help your child with separation anxiety disorder, but it may not be enough, especially in a family-breakdown situation. Some children with separation anxiety disorder need professional intervention. Assessments carried out by CAFCASS for the court or by Expert Witnesses will establish whether your child is one of these.

WILLING CHILD, RELUCTANT PARENT

Almost all the parents who avoid or abandon contact with their children are fathers. Not only are there very many fewer non-resident mothers, but those few are very much more likely to stay in touch with their children year after year and through thick and thin.

If a non-resident father doesn't want to see his child, or even have indirect contact with her, there is nothing the mother can do to make him. He is legally obliged to pay 'child support', but that's only money, it's nothing to do with emotional support or a personal relationship. It seems ironic that a mother is legally obliged to encourage even the most reluctant children to have contact with their willing fathers, but has no legal support for keeping willing children in touch with unwilling non-resident fathers.

Many of the men who have no contact with their children had no more than passing contact with the mothers. If the two parents never lived together and the father only saw the baby a few times (or not at all), his vanishing act will not affect the child as badly as being deserted by a father who is known and loved. Don't assume, though, that a child you have brought up as a single mother will not want to know who his father is and why he didn't stick around. Some mothers who marry within a year or two of the child's birth wonder if it is necessary for him to know that his stepfather (who may become his adoptive father) is not his biological father. All the evidence is that when you judge the child old enough, he should know the truth. It is not only necessary because we all need to know our backgrounds and where we came from, but also because lies within families almost always come out. If your child one day discovers (perhaps because you and his stepfather eventually separate) that the man he has always called Daddy is not his natural father, he will feel that the whole of his childhood has been thrown into uncertainty and everything he knew or felt about his family was false.

The next largest group of vanishing fathers consists of the many whose parenting after separation is not mutual or polite but broken and eventually non-existent. These are often men who get so worn down by the difficulties of negotiating with their exes and keeping to contact schedules with their children that they give up. Often, regular weekends gradually become irregular invitations, and daytime or holiday visits become unpredictable and rare. Eventually they just don't happen any more. For a while – and especially if mothers keep pressing for contact – the easier kinds such as phone calls and texts may carry on. But a vicious circle operates such that, as contact dwindles, it becomes more effortful and therefore dwindles further. What do you say in a quick text to a fourteen-year-old you haven't spoken to in six months?

I haven't seen my dad since I was thirteen. For the longest time – like years – I went on being thrilled when he turned up and believing his excuses when he didn't. My mum was really good about that. But then there was a birthday when he didn't even send a card, and then another birthday, and then I sort of realised he'd gone. I wish I knew where he's gone because I really need to ask him what I did to make him just not care about me.

Boy, now aged sixteen

The last group of vanishing fathers – and thankfully the smallest – consists of men who, however agonising they find the decision, just decide to go. Some of them leave the country and make a new kid-free start. Some of them have girlfriends who wouldn't want anything to do with a child from an earlier relationship. Some of them hope that if they stop seeing you and the children, they can stop paying. Not all these vanishing fathers jump out of their children's lives entirely of their own accord, though. Some of them are worn down by ceaseless criticism and disapproval, low-level alienation perhaps, from their exes. Some are so saddened by repeated rejection by their children that they cannot bear to keep pushing themselves forward. A few let themselves be pushed out by the children's mothers because they do not realise that they can seek help with access from the court, or cannot face a continuing struggle (see page 88).

However it comes about, the loss to children whose parents vanish is almost worse than an actual bereavement. If a father dies (unless by his own hand) it's not because he wanted to leave, and even children, guilt-prone though they are, cannot believe that it's their fault he had a heart attack or crashed his car. But if a father just leaves, it is obviously because he chooses to, and the fact that he made that choice tells his child that she is somehow to blame: she wasn't clever enough or good enough; she wasn't loveable enough or didn't tell her father that she loved him often enough. Grief and guilt is a toxic combination, and most mothers really struggle to find an alternative set of explanations for the heartbroken child that makes sense but is less painful. When she says, 'Why doesn't Daddy come and see me or ring me up any more?' there isn't an answer that won't hurt. If it's clear that your ex really has dumped the child, you probably can't do better than explain that when things have gone very wrong for people they sometimes feel that they have to get themselves out of it however they can and without thinking about how much other people will be hurt. You might want to say that behaving that way isn't admirable but it certainly doesn't suggest that the child has done anything wrong. If you think your child is old enough to want to understand a little more, you might want to add that the only two people who were responsible for things going wrong and breaking up the family were his father and yourself, and that you apologise on behalf of both of you for not having managed to stay together or to separate better.

Being in contact with both parents gives children a sense of security as well as of their own identity. When one parent doesn't wish to be involved in the child's life, knowing about him is almost always better than nothing. Try to make it clear to the child that you are able to talk about her father without getting too distressed, and make sure that she has photos of herself with her father, even if the most recent ones date from years back. If you can manage to remain on friendly terms with your absent ex's extended family, contact with her paternal grandparents may help too.

One day your children may decide to try and trace their other parent, just as many adopted children do. In the same way as it's tough for adoptive parents to see a child going all out to find someone who's had no contact with her for eighteen years, during which they have been loving and caring for her, so watching your beloved child trying to trace a vanished dad who walked out on him, leaving you to be mother and father in one, can leave you seething with sorrow and resentment. Try, though, to work through all those bad feelings and come up feeling good about yourself, because if your child finds his dad, he may get rejected all over again and then he will desperately need your support.

PART III: WHAT WORKS AND WHAT DOES NOT

CHAPTER 9

MORE ISSUES PARENTS RAISE

Parents who separate often have to face practical and emotional problems that none of their advisers had mentioned, and make decisions that they therefore hadn't thought about in advance. Some of them have shared for this chapter the issues that were most important to their children and the solutions they eventually arrived at.

HIGH DAYS AND HOLIDAYS

The routines and rhythms of life as a family with children are punctuated by special occasions, which children expect and look forward to. It's not only the big, personally important days like birthdays, or religious or public holidays, that are important. There are many lower-key 'special days' which your family may or may not have chosen to celebrate, such as Valentine's Day, Mother's Day or Hallowe'en, and occasions that individual families invent and celebrate for themselves, like a special dinner to mark the last night of each school term. Any selection of these – and many others – may have become part of the fabric of your children's family lives, and if family life has disintegrated, what is to become of them? Will the special days carry on now that the routines of daily life that they used to break up are no longer there? Losing high days and holidays may sound trivial, but it doesn't feel trivial to children. Losing those fun punctuation marks in ordinary life that they used to look forward to and plan for will leave holes in children's lives, and finding ways to replace or keep on with them is something that many parents struggle with.

Many parents agree that the best way to rescue the special days that matter most to your family from the doldrums of divorce is to be proactive in changing exactly how you celebrate them. That has to depend largely on your relationship with each other as parents, specifically, whether you can ever be in the same place at the same time so that the children can have you both on occasions that are really important to them, such as a birthday meal. If the two of you being together is a step too far, the following alternative ways of celebrating come highly recommended:

- Instead of trying to make the big holidays such as Christmas just as they have always been but with only one parent, turn out from your nuclear family to the extended family or to your friendship group. Making the ' family' in family celebration into 'extended family' means, of course, that the other parent is welcome to come and take part, and the fact that people from his side of the family are invited should make it easier for him to do so.
- Among your close friends with children in the same age groups as yours it's very likely that there are one or two who are in a situation similar to yours and would welcome pooling support and resources for some occasions. And if you know someone who is completely on her own, an invitation to Christmas dinner at your home would transform the holiday not only for her but also for you and the children, because entertaining guests makes everything different.

Last Christmas was just after we split up and we spent it here, sort of trying to copy the year before. It was horrible. One of the worst days of the whole separation. This year had to be different.

*We don't have family in this country and although friends
invited us, my daughter wanted to be at home for Christmas
Day so we thought, instead of having an empty place at table,
we'll fill it up. We invited an elderly neighbour who has a little
dog the children simply loved, and a young woman who's on
her own with a baby (the children liked the baby too, but not as
much as the dog). She's now my precious babysitter. It wasn't
just a really good day, it was also a day that made me realise I
could still do nice and worthwhile things on my own with and
for the children.*

Mother of girl, aged eight, and boy, aged six

- Birthdays really matter to children and many report being hurt
  or offended by birthday arrangements that were made over their
  heads to suit separated parents.

*The birthday thing made me furious all through my teens. How
dare they say I'd got to stay with Mum for it this year 'because
it's her turn'? My birthday, not anybody else's turn.*

Boy, now aged twenty

If the two of you are ever going to get together to make an occasion
for your children, birthdays are an excellent moment to make the
effort. Some separated parents whose children are school age or
older swear by birthday dinner in a restaurant or a trip to a bowling
alley or skating rink for the child and his best friend(s), because as
well as being a big treat for the birthday child, being in public and
in a formal setting helps parents to be polite.

Summer holidays

Parenting agreements, whether made by the court, worked out with
mediators or agreed privately by parents, usually include the right for
the non-resident parent to take the children on a summer holiday. All

the considerations that apply to overnight or weekend contact with the other parent also apply to going on holiday.

A lot of the problems holidays provoke are general family holiday problems rather than separation problems. But there are real difficulties for one adult taking several children of different genders and very mixed ages.

If you were one of two adults, you could share yourselves out, taking turns so that each child could do the things she liked most and somebody could take the youngest to the toilet, leaving the other playing lifeguard. But as a single parent on holiday with two or three children, you often need to be in two places at once . . .

Some parents recommend teaming up for a holiday with their own parents. Some recommend packages that offer exciting children's clubs with different supervised activities to suit all ages. Many want to go to the seaside, but the fact that children under about twelve cannot safely be allowed in the sea for a single minute without an adult, even if they are strong swimmers (probably in a swimming pool), nor be trusted to stay out of the sea until you get back from taking their smaller sibling to the toilet, makes a beach a highly stressful place for a single parent.

Most parents agree that, whatever type of holiday you settle on, it's easier for two adults to supervise six children (and stay sane) than for one adult to cope with three, which is a good reason to seek out another like-placed family to share with.

PRESSURES TOWARDS INDEPENDENCE FROM ADULTS

As if coping with no longer being a spouse was not difficult enough, the practicalities of daily life as a suddenly single parent can take you unawares and need a lot of organising. Parents say it's more difficult for separated families than for families that have been single-parent for years – or perhaps from the beginning – because post-separation single parenting is a new situation and change of lifestyle for both mother and children and raises questions they haven't needed to address before, many of them to do with whether or not children are old enough to be unsupervised.

RESEARCH

Parents' Views of Appropriate Ages for Children to Be Unsupervised

Average ages given for:

- Walking to school alone: ten years (National Walk to School Campaign gives no specific age – only parents' judgement of child and route).
- Staying home alone for 'a few hours': thirteen years (though some said eight; some said eighteen).
- Minimum age to take a train alone: thirteen years.
- Youngest age for an unaccompanied plane journey: fourteen years.
- Youngest age to be left alone at home overnight: fifteen years.
- Youngest age at which it is appropriate for a child to be left at home for a weekend: seventeen years

H. Thompson, *Home Alone*, YouGov survey, https://yougov.co.uk/news/2011/02/17/home-alone

Being at home alone

Two working parents can usually fill any gaps between their working hours and children's school hours between them. One parent alone must find another way.

I don't know how she'll manage. I drive a cab and I've always been able to take a break to meet the kids from school or pick my daughter up from school clubs and stuff. My wife – I should say my ex-wife – doesn't get home until six, so I don't know what she'll do.

Father of boy, aged nine, and girl, aged eleven

Is this particular child old enough to cope on his own? Will he be all right letting himself into an empty house after school and being there alone for a couple of hours? Or, will she cope with being left on her own at breakfast time and getting herself off to school (locking the front door behind her)?

- There's no legal ruling about the age your child must reach before he can be left alone. The NSPCC suggests that thirteen is the youngest age at which a child is likely to be mature enough to cope with an emergency and therefore no child younger than that should be left 'for more than a very short time'. If a child is under sixteen you can be prosecuted for wilful neglect if you leave him 'in a manner likely to cause unnecessary suffering or injury to health'; otherwise it is up to you – and him.
- A great many under-thirteens from 'intact families' as well as single-parent homes do come back from school to empty houses and occupy themselves until a parent comes home. However, it may be somewhat more of a challenge for your eleven- or twelve-year-old, not only because he isn't used to it but also because it emphasises the loneliness that he is probably already feeling due to the other parent's absence. In fact, an important consideration in this and all other 'home alone' situations is what the child feels about it. A big study of 'latch-key children' in the United States found that a sadly high percentage of them dreaded the time spent alone in the house and many were anxious, even frightened, especially in winter when they returned to a house in darkness.

- It's very unlikely that a child who is not yet old enough for secondary school will cope safely and comfortably with coming home to an empty house. If you are seriously considering this for an eight- or nine-year-old, ask yourself whether you are sure he can remember to take the door key with him, remember also where he has put it, and, above all, easily persuade it to turn. Once in the house, does he know where all the light switches are? Can he get himself a snack? And, above all, can he use a phone? He needs to be able to call you to report that he's safely home and to hear your voice; he needs to be able to phone a friendly adult who is close by (and always in) if he is worried about anything; and he also needs to know that he should dial 999 in any emergency, and that when the person who answers asks him what service he requires, she means 'what's up?' and he should tell her. The harsh truth, though, is that if there really is an emergency – the boiler catches fire, the gale blows a window in or there actually is a burglar upstairs – he will be far too frightened to do anything sensible. If your number is on speed dial he might call you, but you are really gambling on nothing untoward happening; a reasonable bet, perhaps, if he will be alone for thirty minutes; not so good if it will be two hours.
- Two children together are less likely to be lonely and scared, but perhaps more likely to get themselves into trouble, either because they quarrel or because a fun game goes pear-shaped.

The worst was the time I locked Jo in the toilet and then couldn't make the key work. He got panicky so I got the stepladder out of the shed so he could climb out of the window. Only it wasn't big enough and he got stuck. Would I have thought to ring the fire brigade or even the neighbour whose number was written by the phone? Nope. It was pure luck that she heard Jo yelling.

One of a pair of twin boys, then aged nine

A ten- and a thirteen-year-old may be all right on their own for an hour or so, but even the thirteen-year-old should not be expected to look after a much younger sibling

---

RESEARCH

Wrap-Around Childcare

Under the previous UK government's Extended Schools programme, parents were guaranteed a core offer of 8 a.m. to 6 p.m. care and activities for school-age children, and in 2010, 99 per cent of schools were providing access to it, either on their own premises or elsewhere.

In 2015 37 per cent of Local Authorities reported a cut in the number of after-school clubs and 44 per cent reported that breakfast clubs had closed in their area.

Today (April 2017) 62 per cent of parents of school-aged children say that they need some form of before- and after-school and holiday care, but three in ten of these parents are unable to find it.

Check with your local council for information on local childcare outside of school hours, including breakfast clubs, homework clubs and after-school clubs.

https://www.gov.uk/after-school-holiday-club

Some parents find better solutions to the gap between hours of adult work and children's school:

- There may be after-school provision designed for exactly this, or there may be after-school activities that fill the gap while fulfilling a different purpose, such as drama or gymnastics or football.

- If you have good links in the community you may be able to find a much older 'child' – a seventeen-year-old, perhaps – who has exams coming up and a load of homework but is also keen to earn money and would therefore be pleased to walk your children home and stay with them until you get there.
- In some towns there may be a registered child minder who has opted to concentrate on before- and after-school care and has space to include your children.
- If you are very fortunate, there may be a grandparent or other relative or relative-in-law who lives locally, does not work full time and would like to help.
- The very best solution comes with so many 'ifs' that it's rare but: if the children's father lives nearby, his work is flexible or freelance, and you and he are trying to be mutual parents, filling those gaps may be his major contribution to everyone's wellbeing.

Travelling between two parents' homes

If a child is going to move regularly from one parent's home to the other, what's the best way for her to travel? Many parents say driving is the only available option. They suggest that for a short drive two parents should do one return journey each, and for a longer one each should drive half the distance, meeting and transferring the children from one car to the other at an agreed rendezvous.

If the two homes are much further apart, driving may take longer and petrol cost more than public transport, but the car may still score for convenience.

Public transport

If a child or children can travel alone on public transport from one parent's home to the other, parents save both their time and adult fare-money. Parents point out that regulations about how old children must be to travel alone vary from one place and company to another, so you have to enquire.

- **Buses:** Most bus companies say that a child must be at least eight years old before she can travel alone.
- **Coaches:** Some coach companies, notably National Express at the time of writing, do not allow children under fourteen to travel without someone who is over sixteen.
- **Trains:** Children have to be eight years old or over before they can travel alone in trains, and some rail companies say that children between eight and eleven can only travel alone in the daytime (though it's extremely rare to see that enforced). Whether your child is ready to take a train on her own depends not only on her age, temperament and good sense, but also on the line she will be travelling on. Trains that get very full can be daunting and difficult to manage, especially as commuting adults seldom treat children as equal human beings.

> *I wanted to go by train 'cause that way I could go to my dad's every weekend, not just every other if Mum had to drive me.*
> *But the first time it got totally packed and a man said I should give up my seat to a grown-up – 'Haven't you any manners?' he said, and my bag was under the table and I got pushed away so I thought I wouldn't be able to get it . . . I did, but it wasn't fun.*
>
> Boy, aged ten

- **Eurostar** has its own regulations that you need to be aware of if your child will be travelling across the English Channel to visit the other parent. The minimum age for travelling alone on Eurostar is twelve; furthermore, all children between twelve and sixteen years need a 'consent to travel' form from you. Journeys by Eurostar are very long for a solitary child.
- **Planes:** If the non-resident parent moves to a different country, or even to the opposite end of your country, a child's visits may depend on travelling by air. Buying an adult ticket to escort a child is horrendously expensive, but how soon she can fly alone

depends on her age and temperament, the type of journey involved, and your particular airline's regulations and fly-alone service.

BOARDING SCHOOLS

For a child whose parents are separating, there may be a period when 'home' is both emotionally and practically chaotic, with short-notice swaps between the care of mother and father or even emergency arrangements for babysitters or people to do the school run. Most parents realise how damaging these levels of unpredictability and insecurity are for their children, but while most will look for ways to bring stability and security back into the home, some, especially the well-to-do, will consider sending the child away from home to find stability in boarding school.

> *I knew we couldn't go on like that. I meant to be home when she got back from school but half the time I was in the middle of yet another agony-discussion with her father and the other half I was in bed with John.*
>
> *I called in every favour I could from school friends' mothers, but she hates being foisted on people at no notice. And then there was a weekend when John said 'come to Paris' and I actually got a woman from Universal Aunts to move in. Yes, I'm ashamed. Yes, I wanted her out of the way for my sake but truly it did seem better for her too.*
>
> Mother of girl, aged thirteen

Boarding schools have traditionally been seen to provide not only a highly privileged education but also stability and continuity for children whose parents – often in the military, colonial or diplomatic services – had to keep moving so that they would otherwise have had many changes of school. Now stability and security is increasingly sought by parents such as the mother quoted above. People who are separating worse rather than better may neither be able to provide nor allow the other parent to provide a stable and secure home for their children. Boarding school in term-time and holiday visits to both parents may seem to be the answer, but is it?

> *My mother had left my father for another man when I was ten and my father was beyond furious. My mother wanted me to live with her and that's what I wanted too, but although my father didn't want to look after me himself he was determined that she shouldn't. So since she and my stepfather-to-be hadn't married yet, he did a sort of moral outrage thing and forbade my mum to have me to stay in their flat. So I was packed off to boarding school. I didn't know what was happening at home. I didn't even really know where home was. I just felt abandoned.*
>
> Woman, now aged sixty

Sometimes boarding school can indeed provide a safe place and saving routine for children whose home environments are chaotic. For a looked-after child, for example, a carefully selected boarding school can be a good alternative to yet another foster home. Boarding schools have changed, almost (but not quite) beyond recognition, so that older children, especially teenagers whose focus of attention has begun to move from parents to peers, beg to board. Many schools have day-students as well as boarders and will accommodate children staying full time, weekly or even 'on demand', providing all of them with a far less institutionalised environment than used to be the case. Day students often say that they miss out on what their school has to offer if they go home each night. However, other children who go to boarding schools – especially younger ones and those who were sent rather than who asked to go – are shocked by separation and grieve for home and parents.

Even the youngest – the tragic six-year-olds – eventually grow the survival shell that enables them to pretend they are flourishing: 'I was a bit homesick, they say, but it was good for me.' They are wrong. It was not.

If modern boarding schools can be a good experience for some young people, they will not be so for those who are sent away from home because separated parents want their own space and privacy or just cannot think what else to do with them. Such children arrive at school as exiles from the family life they knew before. They feel (and are) abandoned and, very often, that the dissolution of life as they knew it is all their fault and this banishment is their punishment. To make matters worse, the sentence may seem indefinite because where other homesick children can look forward to returning to their familiar homes and secure families for the next exeat, half-term break or holidays, these children do not know what or whom they will go to, or when.

The more muddled the situation is at home, the more important it is that your child should be there so she can see what's happening and, hopefully, see that on some basic level both her parents are 'OK' and still love her.

WHEN ONE PARENT MOVES FAR AWAY

Long-distance parenting is the best that can be managed for one parent in countless numbers of divorced families, because one or the other parent relocates. Common reasons are a new or better job or business opportunity; a transfer or promotion within the current firm; a new marriage or partnership with someone living in another location; moving close to family for support; or wanting to make a fresh start away from the ex-partner.

A long-term or permanent move to a new country is often harder on children than on their parents, whether it is the resident parent who moves abroad taking the children with her and leaving their father as a long-distance parent, or the non-resident parent who moves abroad leaving his children.

Parents warn that whatever the intentions and the promises, long-distance moves inevitably disrupt contact between the children and the non-resident parent. It is not only that many such moves involve enormous distances and therefore demanding and expensive travel for all future contact, but also that, despite the ease and ordinariness of tourist travel between countries, crossing borders, even nearby ones, brings separated parents and their parenting plans up against different legal systems and regulations.

If you want to move away from where your children live, either within the same country or abroad, you do not require permission or agreement from the resident parent, however much she wants you to stay in close contact with the children, and however certain she feels that your relocation will work against that. Your move may go against the contact arrangements in the parenting plan you made with your ex and even against the advice of advisers, but unlike financial arrangements for maintenance, these are not legal commitments.

On the other hand, you cannot make a permanent move abroad with the children without written consent from the other parent. The number of international fights over child custody is going up.

Do be aware of this, because if you moved abroad when consent had been refused by your ex, you would have abducted your children, which is, of course, a very serious crime.

FACTS

Taking Children to Live in Another Country
The number of cases involving parents taking their children to live abroad has risen from 27 in 2007 to a predicted 240 in 2012. Lord Justice Thorpe, head of the office specialising in

international family cases, said: 'We acknowledge, as would all individuals concerned or involved with family justice, the additional emotional distress that is caused to any family by the inclusion of an international dimension. It is incumbent upon anyone who works in such a sensitive area to try and find ways of mitigating such stress, to the extent that it is possible to do so.'

Report from the Chief of the Office of the
Head of International Family Justice, 2012

Even if you are the resident parent, if the contact parent will not agree to your move it will depend on permission from the court. If your application to the court is well prepared, it has a high chance of success, though it may be frustratingly slow to be heard. It may be important for you to warn your future employer, landlord or even partner of the length of time that is likely to elapse before you can travel.

The court will need to be convinced that the move has been meticulously planned, is realistic and would improve the quality of life for the children. It will also take account of the wishes of any child who is considered old enough to put her point of view. If all that is in place, and the court is satisfied that the proposed move abroad is not an attempt to exclude the other parent from the children's lives, it will tend towards granting your application.

QUOTES

'Fathering from afar may, however, become a skill, which current divorce rates make it imperative for men to learn. I was impressed to see Nelson Mandela talking to Arthur Miller on television, shortly after his release from twenty-seven

> years in gaol, describing his efforts to father children he had
> barely known or touched, imparting guidance, boundaries,
> and love.'
>
> N. Duffell, *The Making of Them*, Lone Arrow Press, 2000

Making the best of long-distance parenting

Like almost every situation in post-separation family life, the success of long-distance parenting for children mostly depends on the relationship between their two parents. If the children live with you and your ex is at a distance, 50 per cent of the responsibility for his continuing relationship with them belongs to you. It's even easier for you to alienate the children from a long-distance parent than from one who is close by and around every weekend, and even more important to be supportive.

The long-distance parent will have to work at staying in touch with the children using all the methods suggested earlier (see page 159) and he is far more likely to succeed with your help than without it. For example, you need to be generous in sharing information about what is happening in the children's lives and help them to manage any time differences and establish a schedule for the distant parent's calls. Parents in this situation recommend online programs (some of them developed specially for divorced parents) that allow you to provide information about the children that the long-distance parent can access at any time (and vice versa when the children visit him). Parents who have information tend to be more involved and feel more connected to their children.

The major problem, of course, is the time and distance that makes visits so hard to arrange and afford.

When I first heard that she was planning to go and work in
Hong Kong I didn't think she really would. Take the boys out of

school, out of England, away from me and their grandparents
and all their friends? No way . . . But two weeks later she'd
been offered the job; it was clear she was serious and, well, I
can honestly say I went into shock. After all the grief and work
that went into settling things down after the divorce I was going
to lose them. She thought I might refuse my consent and drag
the whole thing through the courts, but what was the point in
making her hate me? It wouldn't have changed anything else in
the end.

Divorced father of two boys, aged eight and eleven

CHAPTER 10

IN CONCLUSION

This book started with the importance of looking at family break-down from children's points of view, and now it ends there too. There are many books about divorce – this probably isn't the first you have read – but most of them approach it as adults' business when it is very much children's business as well. It's only now, after many years spent researching other aspects of child development and parenting, that turning around the way we handle family breakdown and its impact on children has come to seem both a priority and a possibility. It is a priority because more and more children are being affected, and it is a possibility because recent findings from attachment science show the way.

PARENTS MATTER

The fundamental message of this book is that parents matter even more than is generally taken for granted, and in unexpected ways. That still-growing body of research into brain development offers today's mothers and fathers a new understanding of their own and each other's importance. This is the first generation of parents in a position to realise that from birth, or even before, a child's attachment, first to the mother (or her substitute) and soon also to the father, is responsible not only for his health and happiness today – which is obvious – but also for his entire growth and development as a person, brain and body, now and forever – which is not obvious at all.

Mothers matter most at first

Everything that happens in people's development depends on what happened before, so whatever the age of a child you are concerned for, new knowledge of infancy, the starting point, is vital.

Significant experiences begin to impinge on that development while a baby is still in his mother's womb, which is why at the very beginning of his life she is uniquely important to him.

Once he is born, a baby's primary attachment figure can, of course, be his father, but it will usually be his mother because her relationship with the baby is already ongoing. She and her baby communicate without words or conscious thought, using facial expressions, different emotionally loaded tones of voice (including motherese) and a lot of touching, gesturing and hugging.

All this baby-stuff that used to be taken as much for granted as petting a puppy, and even rationed for fear of 'spoiling', is now known to be enormously important to a child's development. A baby's right-brain cannot grow and develop fully without these intimate human experiences. They are what get imprinted into his brain's circuits. And how a mother provides those experiences for him largely depends on the emotional experiences that were imprinted and stored in the circuits of her right-brain when she was an infant with her mother. These nonverbal communication skills that we learn in infancy are used throughout our lives in all our interpersonal and intimate relationships, including romantic or marital partnerships. And their patterns tend to repeat across generations. Family breakdown often contributes to disturbed childhood attachment, but childhood attachment stressors also play a big part in divorce and the custody battles that so often follow.

Fathers soon matter just as much

It is because a baby's primary attachment starts in the womb and is almost always to his mother that accounts of infant development tend to read as if mothers are the primary parents and fathers secondary. That is a misreading. Over a lifetime, a child's relationships with each parent are equally important, but they are different both in timing and in kind. In the first year what babies need most is maternal regulation of otherwise uncontrollable emotions: soothing and reassurance. But as long as the father is sufficiently available, the baby will be gradually building an attachment to him that will intensify in the second year, when physical exploration and understanding of the physical world come to the fore, supported by new experiences and challenges provided by father's attention and play.

Parental separation is worst for the children

Fresh understanding of the full extent of both parents' importance to their children throws the significance of family breakdown into sharp relief. Parental separation or divorce is very seldom pain-free for anyone, but because relationships with parents are central to every aspect of children's lifelong development, it is most damaging to them.

Parents sometimes assume that babies who are too young to understand what is going on are too young to be damaged by it, but a baby's relationship with that 'primary attachment figure' (usually, though not always, Mum) is the most important aspect of his world, and anything that upsets or distracts her will impinge on him, even before he is born. At the other end of childhood, parents should not congratulate themselves on delaying a long-planned separation until the children are old enough to 'understand'. What those adult children are likely to take from their parents' long-delayed separation is that their personal history was built on lies and that their childhood memories and sense of identity are false.

There is no sub-text in these pages suggesting that, because family breakdown is so damaging, parents should stay together 'for the sake of the children'. An unhappy partnership held together only by duty is unlikely to last for long in our current 'me culture', where personal fulfilment is almost a duty, and is unlikely to make for good parenting or happy children in the meantime. If the relationship between parents has become permanently joyless or intolerable to one or both of them, it will be a chilly environment for their children today and will model loveless relationships for them as they grow up.

PUTTING CHILDREN FIRST

We have to accept separation and divorce as closure to failed cohabitation and marriage. Contemporary society, where many people live into their eighties, cannot manage without it. But the wellbeing of the children who will grow up to form that society in their turn is being put at unnecessary risk by the way that safety valve is deployed. It is clear that it could be managed better. Instead of asking, 'Should people stay together for the children's sake?' we should be asking, 'Can women and men who cannot live in peaceful comfort together be better mothers and fathers when they are apart?' The question is rarely asked, because who gets divorced in order to be a better parent? In any case, if it was asked the answer would be assumed to be 'no'. But it is clear that when separating adults can make children's needs their priority, the answer is often 'yes'.

Focusing on the children

There's no escaping the fact that family breakdown is a bad break for children, and for most adults too. But the message of this book is not all doom and gloom. If we are aware of, understand and learn from the same growing body of research that shows how damaging parental separation can be for children, we can also see how to make the best of that bad job for them.

A vital first step is to reverse the adult-centric way parental separation is dealt with, not only in families but often in lawyers' offices and family courts too. When a family breaks down, everyone's energy goes into fighting for or trying to reconcile the interests of father and mother. An important and often-ignored fact coming out of that research is that the children's interests may be entirely different.

MANAGING MUTUAL PARENTING

Treating children as people rather than possessions

Parental separation means a lot of sharing out, and in the name of 'equal parenting' some children get shared between parents like the DVD collection. But children are not chattels. Contact or custody arrangements that seem 'fair' to a parent or to the court may be not just 'unfair' but damagingly wrong for a particular child.

The final lessons these research data can teach take us full circle back to our new understanding of the overwhelming importance to children of their individual relationships with fathers and mothers. They tell us that when a marriage or partnership has definitely ended, what matters most to children of any age is that parenting has not. When relationships between women and men fail, children's relationships with mothers and fathers must at all costs be protected and maintained. Those costs can be high (outside as well as inside a lawyer's office) because, as the many children's voices in this book make clear, the needs and wants of a particular child may be completely different from the needs and wants of her father or her mother, but it is the child, with her whole future development as a person ahead of her, who must come first.

When a family breaks down, what matters most to children of

all ages is not their parents' physical separation but their enmity. The separated parents who do their children most damage are those who fight over them and try to alienate them from the other parent; such parenting is broken. Children survive family breakdown better if parents can confine their adult issues, anger and bitterness to their woman–man relationship, so that their relationship as mother–father can remain polite. But what will best ease the children through their inevitable misery when the family unit is broken is for separated partners to muster the selfless concern for the children that can keep them united in their determination to carry on being, and helping each other to be, loving parents. I have called that 'mutual parenting', and it is the best possible way forward from family breakdown. No longer a wife, husband or partner, but always and forever a mother or father.

INDEX